DATE DUE

DEMCO, INC. 38-3012

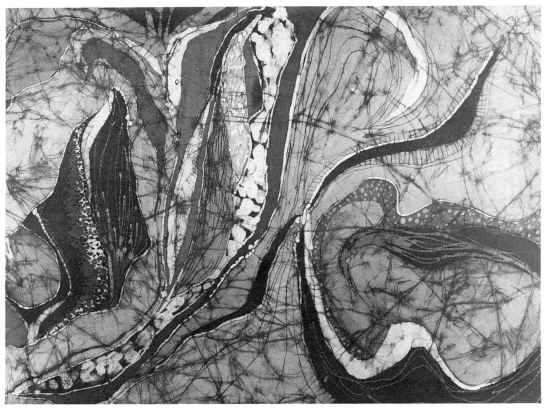

Garden Fragment (35″ × 45″) by Maribeth Frey. Wax-resist batik on cotton.

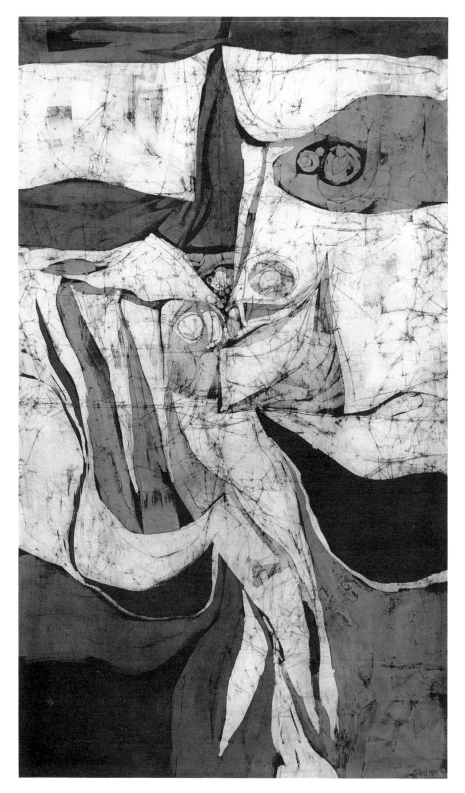

Earth Forms (62″ × 36″) by the author. Wax-resist batik on cotton.

Batik and Tie Dye Techniques

NANCY BELFER

Third, Revised Edition

DOVER PUBLICATIONS, INC., New York

Published in Canada by General Publishing Company, Ltd., 30 Lesmill Road, Don Mills, Toronto, Ontario.
Published in the United Kingdom by Constable and Company, Ltd., 3 The Lanchesters, 162–164 Fulham Palace Road, London W6 9ER.

Batik and Tie Dye Techniques, first published by Dover Publications, Inc., in 1992, is a further revised edition of the 1977 Prentice-Hall, Inc., revised paper edition of *Designing in Batik and Tie Dye*, first published by Davis Publications, Inc. in 1972. An index has been added for the Dover edition.

Manufactured in the United States of America
Dover Publications, Inc., 31 East 2nd Street, Mineola, N.Y. 11501

Library of Congress Cataloging-in-Publication Data

Belfer, Nancy.
 Batik and tie dye techniques / Nancy Belfer.
  p. cm.
 Rev. ed. of: Designing in batik and tie dye. 1977.
 Includes bibliographical references and index.
 ISBN 0-486-27131-5
 1. Batik. 2. Tie-dyeing. I. Belfer, Nancy. Designing in batik and tie dye. II. Title.
TT852.5.B43 1992
746.6′6—dc20   91-48035
                      CIP

Contents

Preface

There are a few links with the ancient past that have not been completely rejected by our immersion in the daily marvels of a mechanized age. These links seem worth caring about and continuing. In different times and in different parts of the world, ideas evolved about using coloring agents. These, together with various other materials, were applied in a manner that formed a protection or "resist" on the cloth. The sections of the cloth so protected would not be colored by the dye; when the resist material was removed, the image emerged.

The hand embellishment of textiles with natural colorants, or dyes, was known to the most primitive of peoples. The resist techniques, requiring the methods of tying, folding, binding of the cloth, as well as the application of penetrating starch pastes or hot wax solutions, were known before the beginnings of recorded history. The uses of dyes and mastery of dye technology are considered by some scholars to be among the more significant achievements of civilized man. In some areas, these skills developed with astonishing sophistication; and then, as religious, political, economic or cultural changes occurred, long-used knowledge became lost.

Many of these processes have been kept alive and today are revitalized by contemporary attitudes about expressive values in art. The traditional examples illustrated in this book give eloquent testimony to the careful complexity of the design motifs as well as the richness of the dye coloration. These pieces are not meant to serve as models to be imitated. They are presented as utilitarian design solutions coming from a particular culture at a particular time, with the symbolic patterning and imagery reflecting very specialized needs and values. We can learn much by studying these pieces, with the realization that today fine skills are most relevant when they allow the artist to pursue his own inventive spirit.

This book describes the historical applications of batik and tie dye resist techniques, as well as a wide range of contemporary approaches and innovations. It is a book for those who wish to learn skills, which are certainly necessary and important. But it is also for those who wish to encourage their ability to see beyond the obvious, to struggle beyond the common-place. Work in these resist-dye textile processes can offer a fascinating challenge, a creative experience of deep pleasure and accomplishment.

ACKNOWLEDGMENTS

A note of thanks is due to my students, colleagues, and friends who helped in many ways.

The traditional batik cloths, dating before World War I, are from the extensive private collection of Mrs. Henry J. Post. Dr. Anna P. Burrell, Harun Arrasjid, and Walter Wells loaned the more recent examples of batik and tie dye from Java and India.

Most of the black and white photography is the work of Stephen Mangione, with special contributions by Paul Pasquarello, Gail Krakauer, Nancy Dayton, and H. Joseph Trapper.

The professional textile artists who graciously loaned examples of their personal creative work for inclusion are Morag Benepe, Marian Bode, June Bonner, Marian Clayden, Carol Parzen, Carter Smith, and for this new edition, Dorothy Caldwell, Kymberly Hensen, and Yukie Orenstein.

Many students from Buffalo State College kindly allowed their work to be used as examples of the various techniques described. Each is individually credited.

1 *Early Uses of Dyes*

Dyes are a kind of magic, a delight to the eye and a joy to use. Even a brief inquiry into the early discoveries and uses of these coloring agents conveys a sense of mystery and glamor. Primitive people in many different parts of the world discovered that certain root, leaf, or bark material could be treated to produce color in a fluid form. Its application was both religious and functional—the embellishment of body, clothing, and utensils.

Ancient Chinese writings, 2500 B.C., mention the use of dyes on cloth. The Peruvians, during a time corresponding to the first centuries of the Christian era, worked with well over a hundred distinct hues in their textiles. The superb mastery of dyeing skills, which developed in India, was praised throughout the Roman world; excavated cloth fragments indicate a tradition going back some 5,000 years.

In Greek antiquity, myths often allude to dye colorings. Of intriguing interest is one of the few truly fast dyes in use at this time: purpura, extracted from gland secretions of mollusks along the Greek coastline. It was known to the Phoenicians and has been traced back

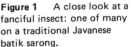

Figure 1 A close look at a fanciful insect: one of many on a traditional Javanese batik sarong.

to Minoan Crete. The term "purple" was applied to the range of red to blue violets made from these shellfish secretions, a colorless liquid that oxidized when it was exposed to air. Hills of crushed shells today identify the remains of extensive dye works. The color was difficult to process and was used only to dye the finest garments, robes, and cloaks worn throughout the Mediterranean world as a distinctive mark of luxury.

Purple has since become a symbol of aristocratic pomp and celebrity, the color of royalty. Strangely enough, knowledge of this color, known as Tyrian purple, became lost during the Dark Ages. It was rediscovered by a French scholar in the middle of the nineteenth century, about the same time chemically made dyes were first introduced in England.

Numerous plants, certain insects and shellfish, as well as some minerals, have been found to be sources of colorants. Knowledge of the preparation and usage of natural dyes evolved slowly over centuries of trial and error experimentation. The formulas and recipes were often carefully protected secrets, subject to cloak and dagger intrigues and trade conflicts among rival countries. In India, where resist dyeing probably originated, the complex technology involved in the formulation of dyes and mordants was mastered to an unparalleled degree of perfection. Indian textiles have been known and prized by Europeans since the sixteenth century.

In the resist-dye techniques, the dyeing of the cloth cannot be thought of as the application of pigment to surface; there must be a

2 chemical reaction between the coloring agent and the fiber so that

the color becomes a permanent, integral part of the fabric. In order to achieve this affinity between dye and cloth, and also to insure fastness and color control, the use of a mordant became necessary.

Mordants are chemical solutions that can be used before, during, or after the dye bath; they prepare the fiber for receiving the color and also control the actual hue obtained. The same dye used with different mordants will produce different colors. Some commonly used mordant substances are organic acids (acetic, tartar, tannic), inorganic acids (sulphuric), and salts (alum, tartar emetic, Glaubers salt). If a certain color is to be duplicated, the preparation of the dye solution as well as the mordant must be exactly the same.

Figure 2   Remarkably detailed, this section of a Javanese batik sarong pictures a proud bird in a garden of freely drawn flowers.

Figure 3 A batik from India, this silk head scarf is in brilliant yellow and red, with stems and leaves in a smoothly flowing surface pattern.

Some of the oldest and most widely known of the natural dyes are:

Indigo—probably first used in India but known throughout East Asia before recorded history. This dye produces the familiar deep blue color so prevalent on Javanese batiks.

Madder—also originated in India; deep, rich reds are produced from powder formed by grinding the roots of the madder plant.

Cochineal—a range of brilliant reds; the grains are prepared from a dried insect, cocus cacti. This dye was first known in South America and Mexico.

From here the list can be greatly expanded to include numerous additional plants as well as certain species of insects, shellfish, minerals, and metals. The ingenious early development of fabric colorants from a variety of natural ingredients paved the way for the complex industrial dye technology we take for granted today. While there is still interest in the preparation of natural dyes, most textile artists prefer working with synthetic dyes in resist-dye applications.

2 The Resist-Dye Processes in Textiles

The various types of resist-dye processes can be best defined according to the type of resist that is used and the manner of its application.

HOT WAX RESIST

Using hot liquid wax, lines and shapes are drawn onto cloth with brushes, special tools, or stamps. The wax penetrates the cloth forming a resist. The unwaxed sections of the fabric are dyed; the sections of the fabric protected by the wax resist remain free of the dye. This process is known as batik throughout Indonesia, India, and the Orient.

In traditional batik, there is a characteristic network of fine, weblike lines scattered over the surface of the cloth, due to the deliberate crushing of the fabric prior to the final dye bath. As traditional methods are simplified and adapted to present-day interpretations, many variations are possible. The fabric can be taken through several overlapping applications of wax and dye, thus increasing the complexity of the design, or the work can be completed with a single application of wax and dye, as in silk painting, eliminating a final crackle-producing dye bath.

Historically, the use of water-soluble flour pastes which are applied to cloth in different ways, is well-known throughout Asia and parts of Africa. In Nigeria, the term *adire eleko* refers to the indigo-dyed decorative fabric made with cassava-flour paste applied with cut blocks and stencils. Other variations include applying the paste uniformly over the entire surface of the cloth, then forming the design by scraping through with a comb or similar tool.

In the impressive textile traditions of Japan, several techniques using starch paste resists of rice flour have been perfected over several centuries. The most familiar are *tsutsugami*, the freehand drawing on fabric with the resist applied through a cone or pastry tube, and *katazome*, in which the resist is applied through delicately-cut paper stencils.

Figure 4   This batik from Indonesia shows the familiar *parang rusak* pattern, a series of diagonal rows of rhythmic motifs developed from the forms of plant and vine foliage.

The term *tie dye* is generally used to identify several related resist-dye processes on fabric that call for different ways of folding or pleating the cloth, followed by the selective placement of bindings, ties, and knots to compress the fabric before it is placed in the dye bath. The tight compression of the cloth in certain sections keeps the dye from entering; the portions of the cloth not compressed receive the dye coloration. The overall pattern emerges when the bindings, ties, or knots are removed and the fabric is unfolded.

Although early examples of tie-resist textiles have been found in many cultures, including Pre-Columbian Peru, these processes are most prevalent in East Asia, particularly Indonesia where the term *plangi* originated. In India the term *bandhana* is used and the elaborate tie dye patterning found on Japanese kimonos is called *shibori*.

STITCHED RESISTS

Tritik, an Indonesian term, is a related bound resist technique in which rows of small running stitches are sewn into the cloth in various configurations to form a predetermined pattern. When the sewing thread is very tightly pulled, the fabric gathers up and compresses, thus forming a resist to the dye. The stitches can be made in straight or zigzag rows, or can outline a specific shape. When the threads are cut and the fabric is opened, the stitches emerge as tiny undyed dots contrasting with the dyed background.

In many examples of tritik found in textiles from Indonesia and West Africa, the stitched resists are frequently combined with other tie dye processes to obtain patterning of great complexity.

CLAMP RESISTS

Controlled placement of resists in clearly defined shapes or figures can be accomplished using clamps. In this adaptation of an ancient Japanese technique called *itajime* or jam-dyeing, duplicate pieces of cut plywood, thick plastic, or coins are evenly lined up on each side of folded fabric and tightly clamped together. This forms the resist; after dyeing, the clamps and blocks are removed to reveal the pattern.

Figure 5   A section of an old cotton batik sarong from East Java.
This is the *pagi-sori* or morning-evening design. Each end is dyed
a different color so that when the wearer changes the folding, the
garment appears to be different.

3 History and Tradition in Batik

Where does batik come from? There is no certainty, but several theories speculate on the origins of this intriguing craft. The word "batik" is Indonesian in origin, but the concept itself was probably first devised either by the Egyptians or, according to other scholars, on the Indian archipelago. It is known that liquid or paste starch resists preceded the use of wax.

In the fourth century B.C., the Greeks invaded India and returned with many textiles. This indicated an already well-established tradition in weaving, as well as cloth painting and dyeing. The images were geometric or highly stylized arrangements of flowers, fruits, birds, and animals; the craftsmanship was of the highest quality. With increasing migration of people and expanding trade routes, knowledge of wax-resist dyeing spread throughout Asia.

About 300 or 400 A.D. Indian traders and merchants introduced the technique to the Javanese peoples of Indonesia, who developed it in their own unique manner to the very high degree of excellence so admired today. Since the textile arts were of great importance to these people, the batiks of Indonesia give us an unusually complete

and unbroken tradition that can be traced for centuries.

Figure 6 A section of *slendang*, a long, narrow strip of cloth worn as a shawl or scarf. The strong linear quality in the diagonal rows is obtained by scratching through the surface of the wax prior to dyeing.

The volcanic island of Java, where the batik art was perfected, was invaded by Hindu tribes from India who remained and were powerful rulers for 1,300 years. During the Medieval period, Arabs came, also by way of India, introducing the Moslem religion. The sultans of these empires were supreme rulers with elaborate palaces and numerous court attendants; they lived storybook lives of richness and splendor. The usual preference for finery throughout Asia is for silk, but the Javanese, because of their ancient batik tradition, favored cotton. Cotton was easy to grow and in a tropical climate, a comfortable fabric to wear. Batik decoration was used only on garments, rather than ceremonial cloths or decorative hangings. At one time a sultan decreed that batik making was a "royal art" to be practiced only by the women of the court. This ruling, of course, could not be enforced for long; the craft was too deeply ingrained among the people, but it serves as evidence of the value and high regard given these garments.

For centuries batik was practiced by the native villagers with a precision and concern for detail that we marvel at today. Time was of no importance; they employed infinite patience, working and reworking motifs handed down from one generation to another. A Dutch anthropologist, traveling through Java over thirty years ago, gives an account of some of these native village practices:

I enjoy a visit to a village. There the meek woman sits quietly on a self-woven mat on the ground before the bamboo frame over which the white cotton is hanging loosely. On her back, tied in a "slendang," a baby lies asleep; other children are crawling or running about the house; chickens everywhere—this is a humble house.

Figure 7   A Javanese woman working on a batik cloth with the
tjanting tool.

At her left is the earthenware little stove, the anglo, on which the
charcoals melt some beeswax in a small iron vessel. She dips the
tjanting, her only instrument into the liquid wax, blows then onto
its thin outlet . . . and finally starts to make her design on the thin
cotton. No pattern, no sketches on the cotton—her heart and
imagination figure design the batik.*

*Tassilo, Adam, "The Art of Batik in Java," *Knickerbocker Weekly*,
August 28, 1944.

Figure 8 (left) A *slendang* or cotton batik scarf with a geometric border design and an unpatterned center. **Figure 9** (below) A section of a cotton batik sarong from Java in the traditional allover pattern of triangular shapes, each embellished with a different motif.

13

History and Tradition in Batik

The women were responsible for the designs and the waxing; the men, for the dyeing and finishing. The ingrained superstitions of many centuries played their part in the ritual of batik work. These skills were thought of as benevolent gifts from the spirits of ancestors. Good work was done only on a "good" day with tools that were blessed. Offerings of incense, rice, and flowers were prepared to win the favor of the spirits. While the waxing demanded great skill, the dyeing procedures were extremely complicated and time-consuming; a slight error in mixing could prove ruinous. If the color was faulty, the evil spirits were surely at work.

Figure 10 A very old but intricately detailed *tjap* or stamping tool.

Figure 11 A Javanese batik worker printing a border design using the *tjap* tool.

All the traditional patterns had whimsical names—"a carefree life" or "moonshine charm"—which assist in identification. Certain patterns were reserved exclusively for the family of the sultan and his highest-ranking officers. These were forbidden for use on other garments. The workmanship and dye coloration had to be perfect; this meant no sign of wax crackle, for any break in the wax meant faulty handling. Batiks with such "defects" had to be destroyed so that the evil spirits would not molest the ruler.

Some aspects of batik making changed when the *tjap*, or copper hand stamp, came into use in Java about 100 years ago. It had been known in other areas for centuries. After the stamp is dipped into a

Figure 12 A portion of an old batik scarf cloth patterned in a profusion of birds, crabs, and sea urchins.

Figure 13 Detail of design on preceding page.

bed of molten wax, the design motif is imprinted onto the cloth. The principle is that of block printing, with the hot wax taking the place of the ink. The stamp was made by inserting the edges of thin strips of copper into a wood base, conforming to a preplanned design. A second stamp was made of the reverse of each motif for printing on the back of the cloth.

This device has obviously made it possible for a batik to be completed in far less time than the *tjanting* method requires. The stamp, which so greatly speeded up the process, marked the beginning of the movement to change batik making from a folk craft or "cottage industry" kind of activity to the small factory type of production that is prevalent today. There are several thousand of these factories in Java today. With some exceptions, aniline dyes have almost completely supplanted natural colorants. The last generation has seen many changes in the social structure which have added to the breaking down of the handcraft traditions that existed, unchanged, for so many centuries.

Figure 14 A young batik worker puts a day's supply of wax into a small iron pot. As the wax must be liquid at all times, it is kept over a small charcoal burner. Djogjarta, Java, Indonesia. An Exxon Photo.

Figure 15 A woman beginning a new batik. She waxes in the intricately involved patterns with a *tjanting*, a small copper container with a long slender spout. From time to time she blows on the tip of the *tjanting* to secure an easy flow of the hot wax. Djogjarta, Java, Indonesia. An Exxon Photo.

Figure 16   A group of women apply second coverings of wax onto
the batiks that have already been dyed in indigo. In the center of the
group is the pot of wax that is kept in a liquid form over a charcoal
burner. These women are all very skilled artists. Djogjarta, Java,
Indonesia. An Exxon Photo.

To the Western eye, the design character of Javanese batiks seem to be bound to a precise scheme of geometric repetition. Although some designs seem more rhythmic than others, there is a lack of dramatic interplay of the motifs. In the culture of these peoples, tradition was very strong—in fact so strong that any deviation from ritual was a moral offense. This attitude was bound to have its effect on the designs of the textiles. The artist as a unique personality was simply of no concern, especially as batik was a folk art, practiced among the villages. There was never a thought of changing intentionally the basic scheme of a design as it was passed from one generation to the next in a particular locality. These batiks should be viewed today on the basis of strong cultural traditions.

SUMMARY OF TRADITIONAL JAVANESE BATIK METHOD

1. Preparation of the cloth
   washed in hot water
   soaked in solution of castor oil or coconut oil
   oil boiled away
   cloth dried in sun
   placed in starch solution
   again dried in sun
   cloth pounded and beaten with wooden hammer

2. Application of the wax
   design drawn on the cloth
   tjanting tool—used to apply wax to outlines and linear motifs
   penembok—tool with a flat, wide spout, used for filling in larger sections
   tjap—a hand stamp, allowing the motif to be printed on the cloth (wax always applied to both sides of the cloth)

3. Dyeing the cloth
   cloth placed in indigo vat until the correct shade of blue is obtained (several days)
   fabric rinsed and dried
   wax scratched away from sections of the cloth that are to be dyed the next color (e.g., brown)
   additional wax applied to the sections that are to remain the indigo blue shade
   cloth dyed in the brown dye bath
   cloth rinsed and dried
       (some sections of the cloth will be blue, others brown; where the brown covers the unwaxed areas of blue, the resultant color is black)

4. Removing the wax
   fabric boiled in water to remove wax

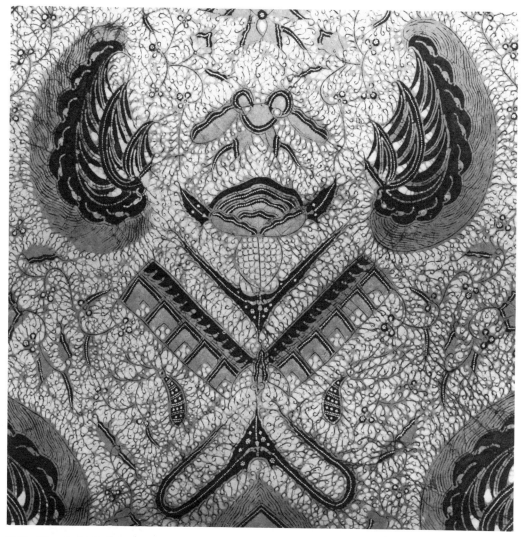

Figure 17 A detail of the "double wing" motif, one of the patterns reserved for use by members of the royal court. This cloth is a 40" x 40" head square, worn by men.

Figure 18　Section of a
sarong with a detailed design
of birds and flowers.

Figure 19 Indonesian puppet. The head, hands, and torso are of carved wood with the features painted in brilliant colors. The skirt is made from a cotton batik cloth.

Figure 20 Detail of a cotton sarong with bird, butterfly, and floral motifs.

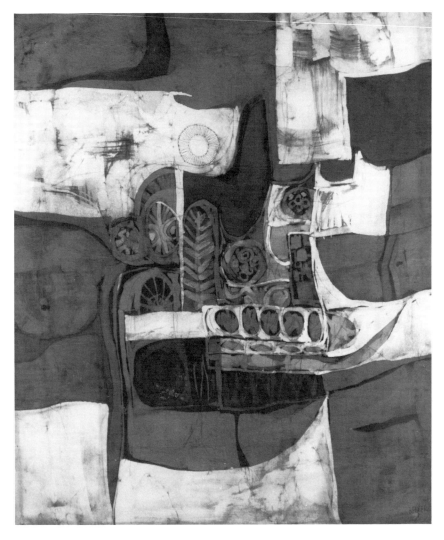

Figure 21 *Entrance View.* Batik on cotton, 54″ × 42″. A contemporary adaptation of the ancient batik technique. In the large shapes, the hot wax was applied with a house-painting brush, 3″ wide. Dyes were applied in both brush and dye bath methods.

4 *Contemporary Design in Batik*

There are certain fairly precise procedural steps involved in the making of a batik. This does not imply, however, that there is a set of mechanical rules to be mastered which, if followed consistently, lead to ever-predictable results. Working within a few basic guidelines, the "how" of making a batik becomes a fluid, personal means of expression. Certainly the nature of the technique is a fundamental aspect of those expressive qualities, but there are opportunities for an unusually wide range of graphic and color effects. Batik is a technique most responsive to the uniqueness of the individual temperament.

As the designer becomes proficient in handling the waxes, tools, and dyes, he gains instinctive knowledge of the variety of visual effects possible. Along with this increasing technical competence, he develops an increasing sense of judgment in building color and form relationships. As in any creative media, mastery of the technical aspects is very much related to the qualitative concerns that often seem so elusive. Because of this, improvisation is suggested for the beginner as the most compatible means of allowing a personal imagery to unfold.

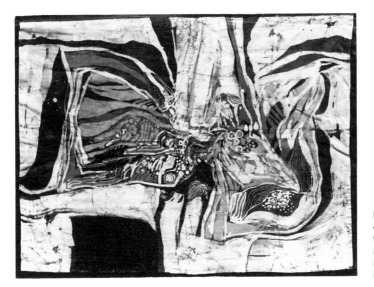

Figure 22 *Habitat* (36″ × 48″), by the author, emphasizes the fluid, linear quality achieved by both the brush and *tjanting* tool. Cushing and Procion dyes on cotton.

The very nature of the batik technique permits a fluid linear quality, as well as the solid shape structures possible when a wide brush is used to apply the wax. With dyeing and subsequent overdyeing, a rich coloration is built that is often reminiscent of the transparencies found in stained-glass windows.

It is important to work in a medium long enough to gain real control in handling it and to understand, through experience, some of its inherent visual qualities. Creative thinking and planning seem to depend on an interaction between this deep knowledge of the material and the kinds of expressive ideas that can be formed by the artist. The more one works, the stronger the grasp of this interaction. When the technical aspects of batik have been understood, they become intuitive, almost automatic; the expressive potential of the medium is then most fully realized.

For example, the line of wax made by a *tjanting* tool has a very different quality from the line made by a brush; the line made by the small pointed brush will be different from the line made by the wider, flat brush. The character and uniqueness of these different kinds of lines are brought into focus by the craftsman, as he masters the use of his tools. When he fully understands what the tools can do, he can use them to best advantage.

While line and shape are the elements first considered in batik, it is color that becomes the most forceful visual aspect of the work. There are many theories about color usage which can be studied; some are very basic, others more complex. A basic knowledge of color terminology is helpful, but effective color planning does not 24 depend on rules.

With some experience, each individual can formulate color harmonies that are personally expressive and do not depend on a predetermined application of scientific theories. There are many factors that cause a color to change visually in relation to other colors used. Therefore, predictable color schemes, when applied to dye usage, can be confusing as well as confining.

Probably the best way for one to begin is by using the colors one prefers by temperament, with the realization that constant and continuous observation and evaluation are necessary. The usual manner of using the dyes in baths is from lighter to darker values. The overall effect is richly unified, since each new dye color intermixes with the previous hue. In direct brush methods, there is greater initial choice of color; the overall effect is bold, full of vibrant contrasts. Here again, with experience, the craftsman evolves his own manner of working, adapting the technique to his own personal requirements.

The batik technique is utilized in many aspects of contemporary creative endeavor. It is found in large murals, permanently installed in buildings; in wall hangings, mounted or framed; divider panels; casement hangings; and as a distinctive embellishment to clothing and a wide range of useful objects. Visually, the effects range from a dramatic personal statement to a rhythmic pattern surface.

For the beginner, the guiding aim is to learn by personal discovery, realizing the uniqueness of one's own way of achieving particular effects, and having the courage to experiment, to try out new ideas. On this basis, serious involvement in the batik process can become an experience of continuing artistic growth and technical confidence.

Figure 23

Opinions will vary among artists working in batik as to the amount of preliminary planning that is necessary. Some feel that thorough planning is essential, with every aspect of the waxing and dyeing carefully worked out on paper beforehand. Others are more inclined toward an approach that allows for a certain amount of freedom to make decisions while the work is in progress. A certain amount of preliminary thinking is always necessary, but a complete colored "sketch" can be very restricting if used as a model to be duplicated in the batik process.

Certainly, an involvement with drawing, painting, or collage making can develop a personal sense of imagery that is essential to creative work in any media. In batik, line and shape formations are the initial design elements considered. Because of this, the quality of the drawing is important even though the medium is melted wax rather than ink, and the tool a *tjanting* or brush, rather than a pen. To think of lines of wax brushed or drawn on the cloth as merely a means of outlining a carefully sketched-in shape is to deny a wonderful vitality and flow of line. The initial application of the wax can convey a sense of spontaneity, of directness and immediacy; this is what gives contemporary batik a far different quality from the sometimes static design effects of traditional pieces.

Sketches are probably most valuable when they are used to give the artist a direction, clarifying the essentials of the idea and providing guidance for specific decisions during the development of the piece. The amount of planning can vary with the temperament and work habits of the artist. It can range from a fairly comprehensive color sketch, to an indication of line and tone, to a brief line drawing, to complete improvisation, working directly on the cloth with the brush or tjanting tool.

The most convenient method of transferring the sketch to the cloth is by drawing directly on the fabric with a stick of soft charcoal. If applied lightly, the charcoal will wash out in the dyes; pastel sticks, however, will leave a permanent mark and should not be used. Working in a freehand manner, the artist can quickly indicate the important aspects of the design, with complex details and variations incorporated as the piece develops.

If a more precise outline is required, as for a geometric design or a pattern calling for an exact repeat of the motif, the paper sketch should be drawn to the actual size of the fabric. The lines can be transferred by the use of carbon paper. This is best done on a sturdy table, since pressure is necessary to go through the carbon paper on to the cloth. If large-size carbon paper is not available, the standard smaller sheets can be lightly taped together.

Another method of transferring the sketch is by using a light box. This can be improvised by mounting a piece of plate glass or sheet of clear plastic over a light source. The drawing is placed on the glass, and over it the cloth; with the light coming through to the cloth the sketch can easily be seen and lightly traced with charcoal.

Some designers prefer to use a tracing wheel, which makes small perforations in the paper sketch. The paper, with these tiny holes outlining the design, is placed over the fabric. When charcoal or light-colored chalk is dusted over the perforations, the lines of the design appear on the cloth.

Regardless of the transfer method used, the initial sketch should be thought of as a guide, providing direction and perhaps inspiration, rather than a finalized concept. There are unexpected surprises in the batik process; new ideas, new possibilities should be allowed and encouraged.

Figure 24 *November Trees* (36″ × 40″). Batik on cotton, dye bath method.

Figure 25 *When the Planets Line Up* by Dorothy Caldwell. (9' × 4'). Wax applications on black cotton; bleach discharge; handpainting. Photo by Dan Meyers

THE STUDIO: EQUIPMENT AND SUPPLIES

Very little equipment is needed for batik work, and a small portion of a room can easily be adapted into a satisfactory studio arrangement. A sink or washtub should be in or nearby the work area. In addition, it is necessary to have:

1. Equipment:
   a means of heating the wax—an electric fry pan, a glue pot, or
     a hot plate with double boiler arrangement
   a sturdy work table
   a wooden frame on which to stretch the cloth
2. Supplies and materials:
   cloth
   wax
   dyes
   dry-cleaning fluid (optional)
3. Small tools:
   assorted brushes
   tjanting tool
   stamps for applying wax (optional)
4. Additional equipment:
   large enamel pans for dye baths
   large, deep pot for steaming
   wide-top jars with covers
   stainless steel or plastic spoons
   rubber gloves
   thermometer
   measuring spoons
   electric iron
   plastic bags and sheet plastic
   newspapers

SUMMARY OF CONTEMPORARY METHODS IN BATIK

The outlines that follow describe, in sequence, three different methods of working in the batik technique. Each procedure has its own unique visual qualities, reflected in the final result. The differences occur primarily in variations in the application of the dyes. (The different methods of application of the dyes are discussed more fully on pages 66-72.)

A detailed series of technical notes (see page 36) describe more completely the specific kinds of information necessary for a thorough understanding of the procedures involved.

METHOD #1 (closest to traditional method)

1. Stretch prepared fabric on frame.
2. Sketch with soft charcoal (Fig. 26).
3. Apply wax to areas retaining the color of the cloth (Fig. 27).
4. Place the cloth in dye bath of first color for appropriate time, rinse, dry (Fig. 28).
5. Attach fabric to frame.
6. Apply wax to areas that are to retain the first color (Fig. 30).
7. Place the cloth in dye bath of second color for appropriate length of time, rinse, dry.

   Steps 5, 6, and 7 can be repeated several more times.
8. If a crackle is desired, crush the cloth prior to the last dye bath. This is usually a dark color. Dry, blotting excess surface dye.
9. Follow dye instructions for fixation; rinse and remove wax.

Figure 26 (above left) Sketching with charcoal on stretched fabric. **Figure 27** (above right) Applying the wax with a brush. **Figure 28** (left) Placing the fabric in first dye bath.

Figure 29 (left) As the cloth dries, the wax appears white. **Figure 30** (below left) Additional wax is applied followed by another dye bath. When dry, the wax and dye procedure is repeated one more time. The last dye bath is a dark color. **Figure 31** (below) Ironing between newspapers to remove the wax.

Figure 32 The finished batik, after three dye baths.

METHOD #2 (direct brushing of the dyes)

1. Stretch prepared fabric on frame.
2. Sketch with soft charcoal (Fig. 33).
3. Apply the wax in areas retaining the color of the cloth (Fig. 34). The design should be planned with self-contained shapes or islands of cloth surrounded by wax.
4. Brush the dyes directly onto the cloth, using different colors in the various shapes (Figs. 35 to 37).
5. Allow time for the dyes to dry thoroughly.
6. Apply additional wax, introducing new shapes or motifs into the previously dyed sections.

    Repeat steps 4, 5, and 6, or

7. Crush the cloth if a crackle effect is wanted, and place the cloth in a prepared dye bath. Dry, blotting excess surface dye.
8. Follow dye instructions for fixation; rinse and remove wax.

Figure 33 (left) Sketching on the stretched cloth with charcoal. **Figure 34** (below) Applying the wax with the *tjanting* tool. **Figure 35** (bottom left) Using a brush to apply the dye between previously drawn lines of wax. **Figure 36** (bottom right) Dyes of different colors are brushed onto the cloth, each shape enclosed by lines of wax.

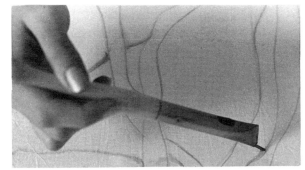

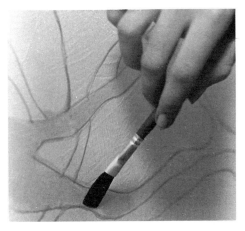

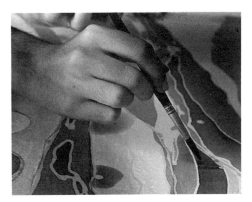

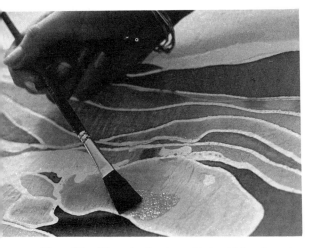

Figure 37 When the dyes have dried, additional wax is applied with a brush.

Figure 38 The cloth is lightly crushed to obtain a crackle effect.

Figure 40 Following the dye bath, the waxed cloth is allowed to dry.

Figure 42 The finished batik.

Figure 39 The cloth is placed into the dye bath.

Figure 41 Removing the wax by ironing the cloth between sheets of newspaper.

Figure 43 Garments by Carol Parzen combine several batik methods. (a) The first dress, in ribless corduroy, has strongly defined dark shapes against a background of heavy crackle.

(b) In the tunic, on heavy cotton, the motif was achieved by folding and cutting paper. Photos by Peter Levin.

METHOD #3 (applying the dyes prior to waxing)

1. Stretch prepared fabric on frame.
2. Sketch with soft charcoal. (optional)
3. Using concentrated dye solutions, apply the color directly to the fabric. Brushes or small sponges can be used. The color will spread; sharp outlines will not be retained. Or, you may apply the color to the cloth using dye paste solutions which are easier to control than the liquids. Brushes of different sizes and sponges are satisfactory. The entire cloth area need not be covered with color.
4. Allow the dyes or dye pastes to dry thoroughly.
5. Using brushes and the *tjanting* tool, apply wax to the areas of color, as well as the background, defining the shapes and organizing the relationships between the dyed and undyed areas of the cloth.

   Steps 3, 4, and 5, can be repeated, or,

6. If crackle is wanted, crush the cloth, and immerse in the last dye bath color for the appropriate time. Rinse, and dry.
7. Follow dye instructions for fixation; rinse and remove wax.

5 How to Make Your Own Batik

THE CLOTH

A medium-weight pure cotton or viscose rayon is probably the best kind of cloth to work with when first learning the technique, but batik can be done successfully on sheer fabrics (organdy, lawn) and textured fabrics (corduroy, velvet), as well as linen and silk. If cloth is purchased at department store remnant counters, care must be taken to avoid any fabric with crease- or soil-resistant finishes. These are chemical treatments that prevent the dyes from properly adhering to the fibers. White or any light-color cloth can be used, with the realization that the background color will affect subsequent dyeing.

The choice of the cloth will depend, to some degree, on the overall character and design of the work. For example, linen is appropriate for strong, bold images that are consistent with the fiber and weave of the fabric. A sharp, clearly defined crackle cannot be obtained on linen; if this final veining effect is wanted, cotton or silk should be used. For wall hangings, smoothly woven medium-weight fabrics are most suitable and can be of any appropriate fiber. Of the textured fabrics, cotton velveteen is especially effective for crackle effects in batik.

Many suppliers of dyes also stock fabric that is free of chemical treatments and finishes. Testfabrics, Inc. is a company that specializes in "print-ready" fabric of various natural fibers that can be used successfully with dyes, eliminating concerns about any fabric treatment or chemical finish that cannot be easily removed.

Ordinary sizing and soil can be removed by washing the cloth in hot water and Synthrapol, a special liquid detergent available from most dye suppliers and highly recommended, not only as a pre-wash but in the final wash-off of dyes in tie dye procedures. This detergent holds loose dye particles in suspension, thus preventing staining of undyed areas.

For cotton and rayon, a small amount of soda ash (sodium carbonate) can be added to the pre-wash. The familiar laundry product, washing soda or sal soda, which was formerly recommended, now contains bleach and should not be used. For silk and wool, use only Synthrapol in the pre-wash.

The fabric can be lightly ironed. Spray starch is optional, but useful for obtaining a clear crackle in the batik.

STRETCHING THE FABRIC

Before waxing, the cloth should be stretched as tautly as possible so that the brush or *tjanting* tool can move freely over the surface. Curtain stretchers, notched adjustable frames, and canvas stretcher frames are all suitable. Frames on stands, designed for rug hooking, are also excellent for this purpose. A frame can easily be made from 1 X 2 pine, joined at the corners and sanded. Small areas of cloth can be waxed with an embroidery hoop used for support.

When you are attaching the fabric to the frame, be certain to stretch only along the grain of the cloth, following a selvage or straight cut edge. Tack the cloth to the frame first at the corners, pulling evenly so that no buckling occurs. Large panels of fabric can be waxed in sections, with the position of the cloth on the frame changed whenever necessary.

Some designers prefer to place the fabric on a smooth table surface, with glass, wax paper, or aluminum foil under the cloth. When the waxing is completed the cloth is carefully pulled away, although some wax is bound to adhere to the base material.

The stretcher frame has the advantage of allowing the wax to completely penetrate the cloth without leaving a residue on the work surface. If dyes are to be brushed on later, the frame is necessary to keep excess color from mingling underneath the work and to permit drying.

If stamping devices are used to apply the wax, the rigid support of a table surface will sometimes give better control as the tool is pressed into the cloth. This is especially true on medium- to heavyweight fabrics, although it is possible to use stamping tools on a tightly stretched fabric.

THE WAX

The hot resist used in batik is usually a combination of two types of waxes melted together: paraffin, which is hard and brittle, and beeswax, which is soft and pliable. The formula is not exact but can vary anywhere from a fifty-fifty proportion to a ratio of three parts beeswax to one part paraffin. If paraffin alone is used, it is quite likely that the wax will chip off the cloth, since it has very poor adhesion and thus readily cracks. Beeswax will not chip off.

Both pure beeswax and paraffin are available from dye suppliers. There is, in addition, a synthetic beeswax or microcrystalline wax available that has the same qualities of softness and pliability as beeswax. It can be used alone or mixed with paraffin as a substitute for beeswax in any proportion. This product, Mobilwax #2305, is much less expensive than pure beeswax and is sold in large blocks of 2½–3 pounds. While ready-mixed blended combinations of waxes can be purchased, it is best to develop an ideal formula through personal experimentation.

HEATING THE WAX

The wax formula is heated to a temperature of about 240°. With some stirring, the different waxes mix together quite readily. The safest and most practical means of heating the wax is an electric fry pan. The thermostat setting keeps the wax always at the correct temperature, thus eliminating any concern about overheating or undue cooling.

While it is possible to use other means of heating the wax, such as in a double boiler over an electric element, using the electric fry pan is the safest and most efficient method. Wax that is not hot enough will not penetrate and appears whitish on the fabric surface. Overheated wax spreads beyond the applicating tool; fumes from overheated wax should not be inhaled. Adjust the temperature so the wax is easy to control and thoroughly penetrates the fabric when applied.

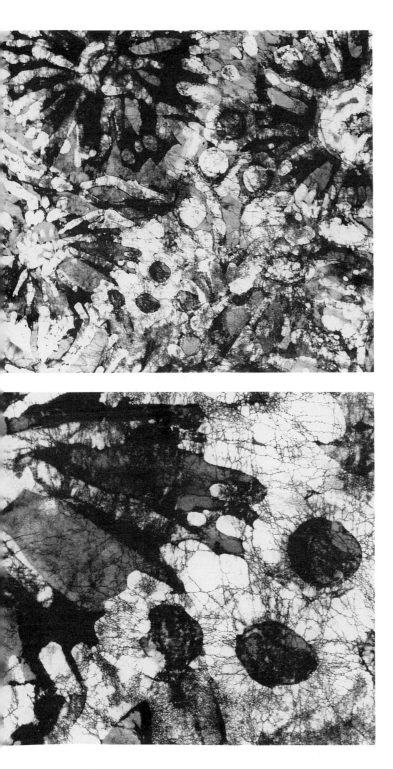

Figure 44 Details from batik
wall hanging, *Red Floral* by
Marion Bode. A richly textured
surface results from crackle
effects on cotton velveteen.
Procion dyes in brilliant reds
and black were used.

*How to Make
Your Own Batik*

Figure 45 *Mexican Eagle*,
a batik wall hanging on cotton
with motifs adapted from
Aztec symbolism. Direct dyes
were used in orange, gold, and
red, with a final dye bath of
black (Marianne Vallet-Sandre).

Intelligent safety precautions should always be maintained when working with hot wax.

1. Set up the work area in a convenient manner so that the container heating the wax is close to the cloth and within easy arm reach.
2. Heat the wax in a container with an electric temperature control unit.
3. If a double boiler arrangement is used, heat the wax in the upper container and the water in the bottom section. Use a stove or hotplate with an electric heating element, never an exposed flame.
4. Do not use dyes or other liquids near hot wax. Any water dropped into hot wax will splatter.
5. Give attention to the wax while it is being heated.
6. When working with students or inexperienced adult groups, carefully explain the need for elementary precautions.

Figure 46 *Floral Theme* (36″ × 40″), a batik wall panel on cotton with warm colors unified by a strong crackle (Nancy Miloro).

BRUSHES

Several flat brushes of natural bristles, ranging in size from one half to three inches wide, are necessary for applying the wax to the cloth. The one-inch-wide brush is especially practical if it has a diagonal cut to the bristles. Sometimes it is possible to purchase this type of brush. If not available, however, one may be made very easily by cutting diagonally across a standard brush with a sharp pair of shears. A fine delicate line can be made with this brush by using the point; wider lines can be made by using the side. The other brushes are used for shapes and textures of different kinds and filling-in of large areas.

The brush is placed in the pan of hot wax. Before it is taken to the cloth, the excess wax is pressed out by running the brush along the side of the pan. This prevents dripping. The brushes need not be cleaned after each use but they should be taken out of the pan of wax before it cools. Although the brush becomes hardened with wax its effectiveness is not impaired if the bristles are not distorted. At the next work session, when the wax is again melted, the brushes should be placed in the pan. After several minutes in the container of hot wax, they will soften and be ready to use.

The brushes can be cleaned by soaking in mineral spirits or commercial cleaning fluid to dissolve the wax.

USING THE TJANTING TOOL

The *tjanting* tool is very closely identified with the Javanese batik. To many craftsmen today, it is considered an optional tool, used primarily for special effects. Its proper use will produce a smoothly drawn line of wax, or characteristic dots and swirls.

Because a little time is required to become familiar with the tool, it is advisable for the beginner to first practice on a spare piece of cloth. The open vessel in the *tjanting* which holds the wax should be filled to about three-quarters, never completely full. This is best done with a spoon, although some craftsmen prefer to dip the tool into the pan of melted wax. The wax should not be so hot that it runs out very rapidly and spreads when touching the cloth surface. It should flow out of the spout steadily, with little spreading beyond the drawn line.

The time factor is important in learning to use the tool with
confidence. Any hesitance or indecision in applying the filled

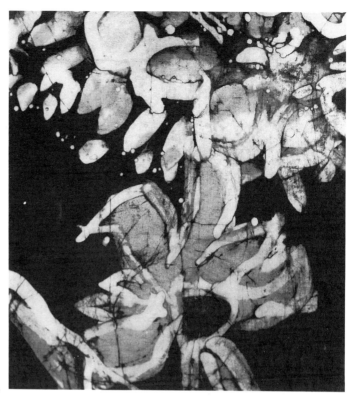

Figure 47   In this batik wall hanging on cotton, brushes were used to apply the wax in a free spontaneous manner. The quality of the brush stroke is always evident, giving character and definition to the forms. Direct dyes were used in both brush and dye bath methods on this large (72" x 36") panel (Sarah Tobin).

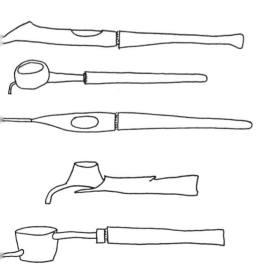

Figure 48   Various types of *tjanting* tools.

Figure 49   Different types of brushes used for applying wax.

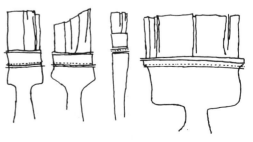

tjanting tool to the cloth will cause the wax to cool so that the line formed on the fabric turns whitish and rests on the surface of the cloth. The wax must penetrate the cloth if it is to provide a satisfactory resist to the dye.

While carrying the *tjanting* from the pan of wax to the batik cloth, drips will occur in even the most experienced hands. To prevent unwanted dots of wax forming on the fabric, hold a jar cap, a rag, or a paper towel under the spout of the tool while it is being moved.

USING STAMPING DEVICES

For more regulated pattern effects, it is possible to make stamping devices which, like the Indonesian *tjap* tool, can press the wax motif into the cloth. Blocks of this type can easily be adapted from objects collected from many sources. For ease in handling, they should be mounted in a small block of wood or fitted with an improvised holder or handle.

Many simple objects can be used directly without any preliminary mounting. Ends of cardboard rolls, wooden thread spools, tin cans with the lids removed, all are readily available and can be used for initial experiments with circular shapes. Kitchen tools and gadgets can also be used as stamps.

More specialized stamps can be made if you cut shapes from quarter-inch masonite board and attach a section of dowel rod or a small piece of wood to serve as a handle. Since the masonite surface is not satisfactory for this type of printing (it absorbs the wax too quickly), a piece of heavy felt of the same shape should be glued to the bottom side. The felt is an ideal printing surface because it holds the hot wax long enough for a careful imprint to be made. Any type of shape that can be cut from the masonite on a band saw is suitable for this procedure.

When planning your stamp, select a base material that will hold the hot wax long enough for a satisfactory imprint to be made. Soft wood, masonite, and pressed board are too absorbent for direct printing; the wax cools too rapidly. For clear prints the surface of these materials must be covered with heavy felt. Metals, however, are excellent, since they retain the heat. Precut shapes of copper or brass can be used, as well as washers and bolts in many different sizes. For a holder attach a 3″ or 4″ length of dowel rod with epoxy glue.

Simple blocks can be made by hammering rows of large nails onto a wood base. The base should be of a size that can be held easily in the hand, thus functioning as a holder. The nail heads form the pattern. The block is held with the nail heads submerged in the hot wax for several seconds. Allow the excess wax to drip back into the container before carrying the stamp to the cloth for printing. Other small objects can be mounted in a similar way. It is necessary to first experiment on small sections of fabric to discover the most effective use of any stamping device.

Figure 50 A group of stamping tools cut from masonite, with felt attached to the surface of the shape. The handles are of wood.

Figure 51 Samples showing different ways the stamping tools might be used (Peter Sloan).

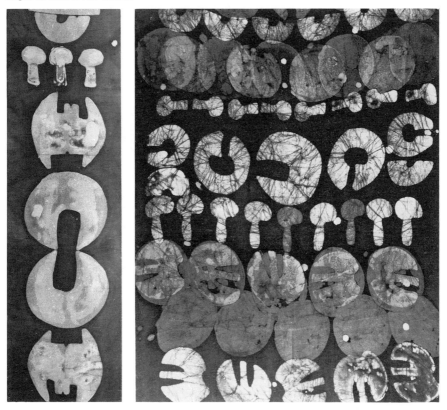

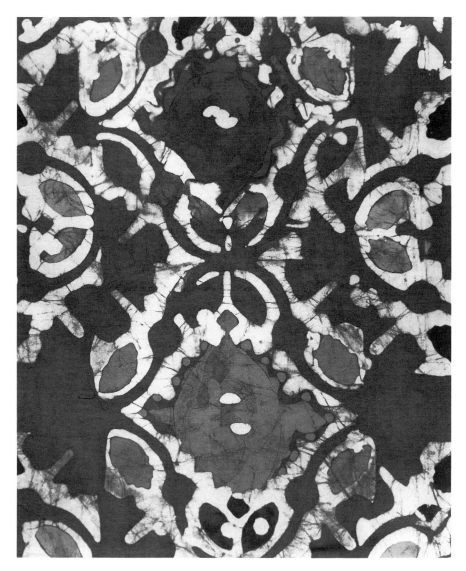

Figure 52 A small Indian wood block was used as a stamp to apply the wax on cotton fabric (Cynthia Bainbridge).

The network of linear markings scattered over the surface of a batik cloth has become so characteristic of the process, it is almost its first means of identification. These weblike lines occur wherever the smooth surface of the wax is broken, thus allowing the dye to enter the cloth. Deliberate crushing or folding of the cloth before immersion in the dye bath will result in crackle formations.

Crackle effects, although used a great deal, should not be thought of as uniform or automatic, since their placement and density can be controlled without too much difficulty. It may be that no crackle at all is wanted; in that case the greater proportion of the wax formula should be beeswax or its commercial soft wax equivalent.

The beginner should be cautioned against too much crackle, because this can overpower the color and shape effects previously established within the design. With some experience it will be possible to control the use of crackle so that it truly enhances the total effectiveness of the work. Regardless of whether or not the dipping or the brushing procedure is used in building the design, the crackle is usually obtained in the last dye bath—in most cases, a dark color.

For a fine crackle, it is suggested that the cloth be chilled, so that the wax will be as hard as possible. If convenient, empty a tray of ice cubes into a filled sink or large pan of water. Place the waxed cloth, folded, in this bath for about five minutes. Cold tap water will suffice if ice is not available. Remove the cloth from the bath and unfold it. To break the surface of the wax, crush it several time from different angles. Do not be overly energetic in doing this or sections of wax may chip off. For a very light crackle, the normal compressing of the cloth to fit the dye bath will probably be sufficient.

Carefully pull the crumpled fabric back to its original shape and gently fold it for immersion in the cool dye bath. At the completion of the dye bath remove the fabric, spreading it out on a bed of newspapers and sponging off excess dye which might adhere to the wax surface. Allow the cloth to dry thoroughly, then rinse in cool water and dry again before ironing out the wax.

LINEAR EFFECTS: FOLDING

If a fairly controlled linear effect is wanted in the batik, it is possible to fold the cloth so that a series of lines, rather than a random crackle, is formed as the wax cracks. These lines are then
47 dyed into the cloth.

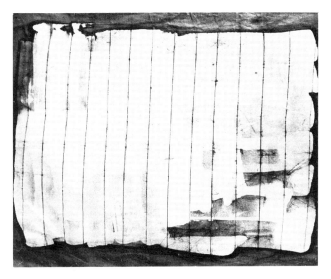

Figure 53 Sample showing fold lines
made in the wax before the dye bath.

The directions for chilling the cloth are the same, but instead of being crushed, the fabric is precisely folded so that the wax is cracked in a straight line. Work slowly, gently firming the fold line as it is made. These folds can be parallel, radial, or variable and of differing directions and lengths. This technique is probably most effective when confined to certain sections of the piece, rather than utilized as an all-over surface effect.

LINEAR EFFECTS: DRAWING INTO THE WAX

Before the last dye bath, it is possible to actually draw or scratch linear markings into the wax, which are then permanently dyed into the cloth. Here again, this is a technique best utilized in one or two areas of the work.

The tool for this drawing or sgraffito can be improvised, as long as the marking point is smooth and there is no danger of accidentally tearing the cloth. A section of ¼″ dowel rod, sharpened to a point and lightly sanded, works very well, as do some brush-handle tips.

REMOVING THE WAX

The removal of the wax is usually done in two stages—ironing and dry cleaning.

The ironing of a large batik (see Fig. 31 on p. 31) is most efficiently done on the floor or on a worktable surface where layers

48

of newspapers can be built up to a thickness of about a quarter of an inch. The newspapers should be at least a week old so the ink is thoroughly dry and will not stain the cloth. Newsprint pads and paper towels can also be used for this purpose. Place the batik on the bed of papers, placing one sheet of paper over the top surface. With the iron set according to the correct cloth temperature, move it slowly over the top layer of paper. The melting wax will be absorbed by the paper. When the top sheet of paper is stained with wax, lift it off and discard it, discarding as well the paper directly beneath the fabric. Repeat this procedure until the papers no longer absorb the wax. (See Fig. 41.)

Figure 54 Drawing lines into the wax with a sharpened section of dowel rod.

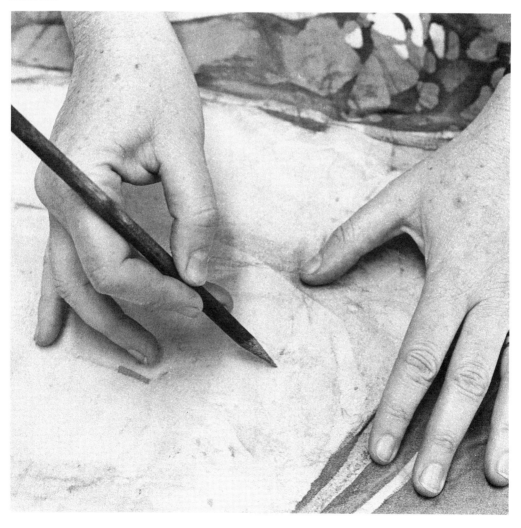

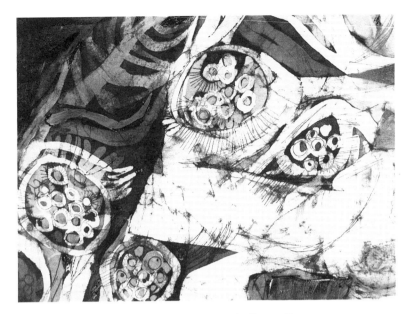

Figure 55   Detail of completed batik showing the linear effects obtained by drawing into the wax surface.

The cloth will be stiff at this point, since the ironing does not remove all the wax. In addition, rings of wax will show on the cloth where a dyed section is next to a waxed shape in the design. To remove all the wax, soak the cloth for a short time in a solvent that will dissolve whatever wax still remains in the fabric. The safest solvents to use for this purpose are those prepared for dry cleaning, purchased from department stores or from suppliers to commercial dry cleaners.

Paint thinners, such as benzine or mineral spirits, can also be used to dissolve the wax but these are highly flammable and must be used with extreme caution, never near an open flame or cigarette.

After using a solvent, do not iron the batik until it has thoroughly dried and the fumes have evaporated.

Unless the dyes used are known to be permanent, it is not recommended that wax be removed by boiling off, since doing so could result in drastic color loss.

If the batik fabrics are several yards long or if a large number of smaller pieces has been accumulated, the most practical solution for complete wax removal is to bring the fabrics to a reliable and agreeable commercial dry cleaner after ironing out as much wax as possible. The cost should be predetermined but it is usually nominal considering the time saved and the effectiveness of the results.

Although it is only since the middle of the last century that man-made or synthetic dye substances were discovered and perfected for use by the textile industry, they have almost entirely replaced natural dyes. Except in some of the most remote areas of the world, methods for growing, processing, and applying natural dyes, perfected over many centuries, suddenly became obsolete. The new dyes were more brilliant, more permanent, less costly, and far easier to use. By increasing or decreasing the proportion of the dye to the weight of the fabric, any hue, tint, or shade could be obtained.

As more and more synthetic dyes were formulated they became categorized into specific types or classes, based on their respective chemical components and their affinity for bonding with only certain designated fibers. There are many classes of dyes but since they are manufactured for the textile dyeing industry, not all types are available for distribution in the relatively small amounts appropriate for home or studio use. In addition, not all dye types can be used safely and effectively with the various resist-dye textile techniques presented here.

The classes of dyes most suitable for resist-dye applications are fiber-reactive, acid, direct, household (a combination of acid and direct), basic, and soluble vat dyes. Fiber-reactive dyes are historically the most recent of the synthetic dyes, first developed in England about thirty-five years ago for use by the textile industry, but they have proven to be the most useful and practical dyes for the textile artist. The original manufacturer, ICI Organics, Ltd., uses the brand name Procion, which has come into general usage to signify this type of dye, although it is now produced by several other companies. Fiber-reactive dyes are available in both powder and in concentrated liquid forms.

In selecting a dye, the first consideration should be given to its affinity to the type of fiber on which it will be applied. Cotton, viscose rayon, and linen are designated as cellulosic fibers; fiber-reactive and direct dyes will have the best affinity. Silk and wool are designated as protein fibers; acid dyes, basic dyes, and fiber-reactive dyes can be used on these fibers, but for wool, acid dyes are preferable. Since household dyes are mixtures of direct and acid dyes, they can be used on both cellulosic and protein fibers. Although acid dyes will work on nylon, in general, the resist-dye applications described here will be most effectively done on cotton. rayon, silk, and linen.

Dyes, like many other materials used by artists and craftspeople, should always be handled carefully because improper use can present a potential danger to health. It is easy to become caught up in the enjoyment of working with dyes, but necessary precautions should not be forgotten. For the most part, these precautions are based on the same kind of commonsense concerns applied to many household items.

Although some dyes are non-toxic, many are manufactured with substances considered to be toxic if they are taken into the body. Even with natural dyes, the substances used for mordanting should be handled with great care. Keep in mind the following guides for using dyes safely.

1. Dyes and dye additives in powder form should not be inhaled or allowed to be ingested through food or utensil contamination. Avoid snacking in the work area and do not store food near the dyes. Dishes, utensils, and pans used for dyes should not be used for food.

2. Wear a protective dust mask to avoid inhaling dye powder when measuring out the dye from one container to another. Some individuals are unusually susceptible to respiratory ailments or dust allergies when handling certain dyes, and should wear a respirator or use dyes prepared in liquid form.

3. Dyes can stain and sometimes irritate the skin. Wear sturdy rubber gloves when using dye baths and thin latex gloves for brush or sponge applications. Remove dye stains with soap and water or prepared hand cleansers; never use chlorine bleach on the skin. Wear a smock or apron while working.

4. Store dyes and dye additives in tightly covered, labeled containers. Keep the work area clean and well-organized.

5. Carefully read and follow the supplier's instructions for using specific dye products. Many types of colorants are marketed; responsible suppliers will provide clear directions and alert the user to potential health hazards.

6. Children working with dyes should be properly instructed and supervised.

Figure 56   *Calusa Totem* (57" × 37"). Wall panel by June M. Bonner.
Wax resist technique using *tjanting* tools, brushes, and blocks on cotton.

53

In working with dyes on fabric, the selection, the mixing, and the application of the color is the most fascinating aspect of the design process. Since dyes are transparent, entering into the thread structure of the fabric rather than coating it, countless tonalities, ranging from brilliant to subtle, are possible by mixing and overdyeing. Color is the element that communicates the essential spirit and mood of the design. It attracts and draws the viewer into the experience of appreciation that encompasses all of the other visual qualities present in the work.

A formal study of color can lead to investigations of several scientific theories, each valuable and informative. When we work with color as artists, however, the theories that intellectually explain how to devise harmonious combinations of colors are of less importance than the development of a personal awareness of color and the striking, yet subjective, impact our color choices have on our work. Using color effectively does not depend on following predetermined color schemes. The instinctive sensibility needed for selecting colors that work well together and convey our expressive intentions needs to be developed along with the mastery of technical skills. It is only through extensive trial-and-error experimentation with color that a truly personal palette emerges.

PRIMARY COLORS

Information about color and color mixing is usually based on the familiar color wheel and the three primary colors of red, yellow, and blue. In theory, all colors can be produced from these primaries. In actual practice, however, the resulting mixtures are seldom satisfactory.

Perhaps you have tried to mix a brilliant green by combining primary yellow and primary blue and found that the resulting green was dull rather than bright; or you have tried to mix a brilliant purple by combining primary red and primary blue and found that the resulting purple was far less intense than expected. It is apparent that the traditional primary colors are not satisfactory as a basis for mixing dyes and other colorants. Another system is needed.

In commercial color process printing, used to print illustrations in books and periodicals, only four colors of printing inks are used, from which all the other colors needed are mixed, three primaries and black. The primary colors are:

        magenta—sometimes called cerise or fuchsia

        yellow—pure lemon yellow

        turquoise—sometimes called cyan or peacock blue

Figure 57   The poignant nostalgia of three aging ladies in a chorus line is expressed by Diane King in this batik wall hanging, *Three Dancers.* Procion dyes were used on cotton.

This is the best system to use when mixing colors with dyes. The mixtures will be bright and can be dulled or darkened later, if desired. With a set of box watercolors (12 or 16 colors) and two brushes, practice simple color mixtures using the printer's primaries, observing how unequal amounts of each component change the result.

When selecting dye colors for purchase it is obviously not necessary to order every available color. On suppliers' color charts, each color is usually named and coded by number. Study the charts carefully to determine which colors are closest to the designated primaries. If you enjoy the challenge of color mixing, it is possible to work only with magenta, lemon yellow, turquoise, and black. A broader grouping of basic colors includes:

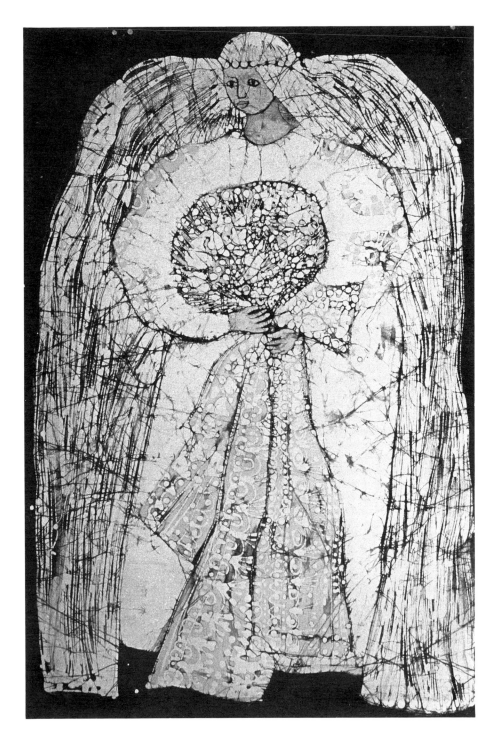

Figure 58   In the wall hanging, *Bride*, Morag Benepe utilizes to
best advantage the unique textural qualities of the wax to portray
the poetic white-veiled figure.

Reds:	magenta (fuchsia, cerise)
	scarlet red or true red
Yellows:	lemon yellow
	golden yellow
Blues:	turquoise
	ultramarine, royal, or navy blue
Black:	for darker values in all colors
	for mixing grays

From this grouping it is possible to mix countless variations. To darken a color, add small amounts of black or navy blue. When a small amount of black or navy is added to yellow and orange, unusual tones of olive and brown result. The richest browns are obtained from an orange base with additions of various blues, turquoise, and greens. To obtain lighter colors, simply decrease the proportionate amount of dye to the water. Since colors always appear darker when wet, always test color mixtures on scraps of the same fabric used for the project.

After some experience working with dye mixtures, certain favorite colors will emerge as important to the overall palette. These can be purchased premixed, if available, for convenience and ease of use.

DYE APPLICATIONS FOR BATIK

The classes of dyes described will be appropriate for the two methods of application used in batik, immersion dye baths of the entire fabric and direct applications of the color in selected areas outlined by the wax. Both methods can be used in the same work, depending on the color effects considered most suitable for the design. Directions for preparing the immersion dye baths and recipes for mixing the concentrated solutions for hand painting will vary with each specific dye.

Although most dyes are packaged in powder form, some are now available in liquid form as well. Some dyes require heat, so the dye bath must be cooled to 100°–110°F. to keep the wax from melting, while other dyes are formulated to work at room temperatures. Each type of dye has certain advantages and in some cases, disadvantages, pertaining to ease of use, fastness to light, washability, and affinity for the particular fiber selected for the work. The relative importance of these criteria determines the choice of the colorant.

When using dye powders, it is necessary to first "paste" or thoroughly mash the measured amount of dye in a small amount of cool water. Using a flat stick, a small spatula, or a spoon, stir the mixture carefully to completely dissolve all of the color particles. Then add additional water, either hot or cool, as the directions require, along with the designated additives appropriate for each type of dye. Soft water is important to successful dyeing, so add Calgon to the dye bath in the approximate amount of one teaspoon to each quart of liquid if you live in a hard-water area.

Enamel or stainless steel pans or kettles large enough to accommodate the fabric are needed for dye baths. Aluminum and galvanized metal will corrode, including small chips in enamelware which will rapidly open into holes. Plastic pans and pails can be used for room-temperature dye baths as well as for rinsing.

Dye mixtures for hand painting are best stored in glass or plastic jars with fitted lids. Self-stick labels are convenient for identifying the dye type and the proportions of the colors used in the mixture. Also note the date, since some dyes have a limited storage life after being activated.

Other items needed include a set of plastic or stainless steel measuring spoons, measuring cups, a funnel, a kitchen thermometer, rubber gloves, and a dust mask if recommended by the supplier or if you are susceptible to dust allergies or respiratory problems.

In describing the various dyes, specific brands are mentioned as representative of each type, but not necessarily exactly the same. Complete addresses will be found in the suppliers' listing.

FIBER REACTIVE DYES

DESCRIPTION: Fiber-reactive dyes have the highest ratings for fastness to light and washability because of the permanent molecular bond of the colorant to the fiber. The colors are clear and brilliant, with affinity for cotton and rayon in dye baths and solutions for direct painting applications, and can be used on silk as well. The dyes are activated by a strong alkali, soda ash, in dye baths; hand painting solutions are prepared in a base of "chemical water" activated by the addition of baking soda just prior to use. After the activator is added, the dyes must be used within a given time span, which varies somewhat with different brands.

DYE BATHS: Warm tap water is used for the dye bath, in an amount just enough to cover the immersed fabric. Proportions are approximate. For a one-gallon dye bath, use:

> 2–4 teaspoons pasted dye (medium shade)
> 1 cup salt (dissolved in hot water)
> 1 teaspoon Synthrapol
> 1–2 teaspoons water softener (optional)

Enter the fabric for 10–15 minutes, then stir in:

> 2 tablespoons soda ash (dissolved)

Continue for 30–60 (or more) minutes, turning the fabric frequently.

Rinse off excess dye with cool water to protect the wax.

In rinsing, there is frequently a great deal of excess dye that does not fix to the fiber and washes away. A dye bath of soft water will somewhat counter this tendency of reactive dyes to "hydrolize" but it should be expected to some degree and may leave the resulting color on the fabric lighter than anticipated.

Figure 59   *Shoes* (22″ × 22″). Batik
on cotton without surface crackle.
The dyes were hand painted following
tjanting tool wax applications.

In the batik process, it is important to realize that with fiber-reactive dyes, the wax does not hold firmly in the fabric during the dye bath because of the strong alkali content of the dye bath water. A pH reading of 10.5 is needed. A greater proportion of beeswax or microcrystalline wax to paraffin (or no paraffin at all) in the formula will help somewhat but repeated dye baths on the same fabric are not recommended. A solution is to use fiber-reactive dyes for direct hand painting applications in the wax outline method and, if a final dyebath for crackle is desired, use direct dyes or household dyes.

PAINTING SOLUTIONS: Fiber-reactive dyes are excellent for use in hand painting solutions in the wax-outline batik method on cotton, rayon, and silk, applied with brushes or sponges while the fabric is stretched taut. A "chemical water" or painting medium is first prepared as a base to which the dye is added in varying amounts, depending on the desired depth of color. Bicarbonate of soda (baking soda) is added as a fixative prior to application. Using a one-quart plastic container, add:

> 1 cup urea dissolved in 2 cups hot water
> 1 tablespoon water softener
> 2 cups cold water; stir.
> For ½ cup hand painting solution, pour the chemical water into a container, add the pasted dye in the amount needed, stir in 1 teaspoon baking soda.

With some types of fiber-reactive dye, the addition of a color enhancer called Ludigol or Resist Salt L is recommended to insure maximum color richness on silk, particularly in achieving deep shades of navy and black. Whether purchased in liquid or flake form, add the correct proportional amount to the chemical water suggested by the supplier.

Thickeners (sodium alginate) can be added to the hand painting solution to prevent the color from spreading. If additional wax is applied over the hand painted areas to increase the complexity of the batik design, be certain the dyes have thoroughly dried, since any dampness in the fabric will cause the wax to chip off.

Hand applications of dye need to be fixed to the fiber prior to rinsing, by steaming or an alternative method. In the chapters reviewing painting on silk and tie dye, variations in the use of fiber-reactive dyes pertinent to these techniques will be described.

BRANDS:	Procion MX	Aljo Reactive
	Procion H	Createx Liquid
	Pro Liquid	Cibacron/Fibracron

DESCRIPTION: Direct dyes are especially formulated for use on cellulosic fibers: cotton, viscose rayon, and linen. The color range is excellent, and intermixing can extend even further the number of hues obtained. Direct dyes require only the addition of salt as the exhaust agent. The colors are reasonably fast to light, but should not be subjected to boiling or hard washing.

Unlike fiber-reactive dyes, which will bond in warm water with a fixing agent, direct dyes require a hot simmer bath for yardage dyeing. When used for dye baths in batik work, the temperature of the dye bath should be cooled to 110°F. to keep the wax from melting. To compensate for the cool bath, the amount of dye used is increased, and the length of time is extended.

Direct dyes do not require additives, such as soda ash, which dislodge the wax in the dye bath, an important advantage in batik since unwanted chipping and breaking of the wax is detrimental to the design. Direct dyes can be used safely for successive dye baths as well as final dye baths for crackle effects.

DYE BATHS: Select a container large enough for the fabric to be gently moved about without crowding. Proportions given are approximate. For a one-gallon dye bath, use:

> 1 teaspoon pasted dye
> 1 cup hot water to dissolve the dye
> 5 tablespoons salt (dissolved)
> 1 tablespoon water softener
> Warm water as needed for the bath

For batik, check the dye bath temperature. Enter the prewetted fabric, moving it about frequently during the course of the dye bath, which can extend from 30 to 60 (or more) minutes. The color appears much darker when wet; a corner of the fabric can be ironed dry to check the color depth. Rinse in cool water.

PAINTING SOLUTIONS: A concentrated solution for hand painting on cotton and rayon can be made and stored in an 8-oz. jar with a lid. Use ½–1 teaspoon pasted dye, 1 teaspoon each of salt and water softener. Add boiling water and stir. Use while warm. Stored solutions can be warmed with an electric coil immersion heater.

BRANDS:	Aljo Direct	Dual Component:
	PRO Diazol Direct	Cushing
		Deka Series L
		RIT

How to Make
Your Own Batik

DESCRIPTION: Acid dyes are formulated specifically for use on protein fibers—silk and wool—although they can also be used on nylon. The colors are brilliant. Fastness to light is good; washability is limited to hand-washing in cool water with a non-alkali detergent. The addition of acetic acid is used to exhaust the dye. For economy, purchase acetic acid in a 56% solution; white vinegar, which can also be used, is only a 5% solution so much more is needed proportionally.

Figure 60   Detail of large wall hanging using direct and basic dyes on cotton (Lucille Licata).

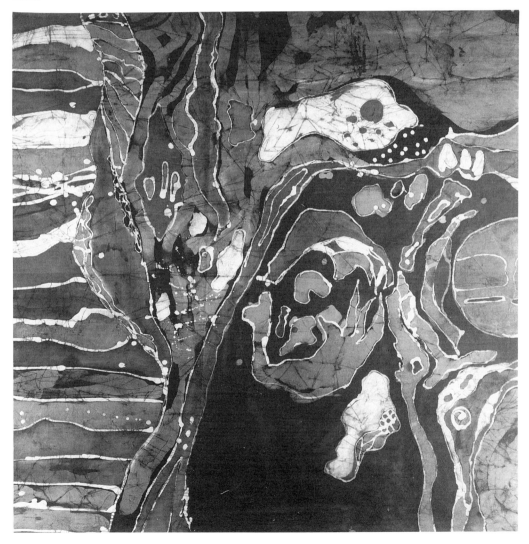

Figure 61 Decorative fabric patterned in soft gold tones with orange. Acid dyes on silk (Carol Edwards).

DYE BATHS: Acid dyes, like direct dyes, require a lengthy hot simmer bath for yardage dyeing, so for the cool dye bath needed for batik applications the amount of dye used is increased and the length of the dye bath time extended. Proportions given are approximate.

For a one-gallon dyebath use:

1 teaspoon pasted dye

1 cup hot water to dissolve the dye

3–5 tablespoons salt (dissolved)

2 tablespoons 56% acetic acid for silk (more acid is needed for wool)

Additional warm water as needed

For batik, check the dye bath temperature. The prewetted fabric should be moved about frequently during the course of the dye bath, which can extend from 15 minutes for a pale color on lightweight silk to an hour or more, depending on the density of the fabric and the depth of color. The leftover dye bath can be reused for a lighter color or mixed with another color, with the addition of more acid.

PAINTING SOLUTIONS: A concentrated solution for hand painting on silk can be prepared and stored in an 8-oz. jar with a lid. Use ½–¾ teaspoon pasted dye, 1 tablespoon dissolved salt, and 2 teaspoons 56% acetic acid. Add boiling water and stir. Use while warm.

NOTE: Lanaset or Telana dyes are acid dyes that require a different procedure from the one described here. Liquid acid dyes and ready-to-use fabric paints are available for direct painting on silk, in addition to the powdered acid dyes reviewed here. These are described on pages 82 and 83.

BRANDS: Aljo Acid Dyes
Ciba Kiton
Pro Acid Dyes

HOUSEHOLD DYES (DUAL-COMPONENT DYES)

DESCRIPTION: Household dyes, sometimes called union dyes, contain portions of two distinct classes of dye, direct and acid, enabling them to be used successfully on both cellulose and protein fibers. The dyes can be used on cotton, rayon, silk, and wool, but depending on the fiber selected, only that portion of the dye which has the correct affinity will be absorbed into the fabric permanently; the unused portion of the dye is rinsed away. Since a portion of these dyes is wasted, they are somewhat more expensive than other fiber-specific dyes but their convenience and versatility is an advantage in some circumstances.

The light-fastness and washability follow the descriptions previously given for direct and acid dyes.

DYE BATHS: The dye bath directions for batik on cotton require the addition of salt, and those for silk call for the addition of acetic acid or vinegar. Brands will vary somewhat regarding the dye bath additives, so it is necessary to review specific instructions, but in general, the procedure is similar to that given for direct and acid dyes.

PAINTING SOLUTIONS: Concentrated solutions for hand painting will also follow the directions previously given for direct and acid dyes. They can be intermixed and stored in the same manner.

BRANDS: Deka Series L
Cushing
RIT

BASIC DYES

DESCRIPTION: Basic dyes have an affinity for silk and wool and are used for painting on silk. For use on cotton and rayon, a prior mordant bath is required to establish affinity. Basic dyes produce unusually brilliant, vibrant colors when compared with other dyes, but unfortunately the colors fade after a period of exposure to natural light.

While these dyes are suitable for certain special color effects or articles not generally exposed to sunlight, they are not generally avail-

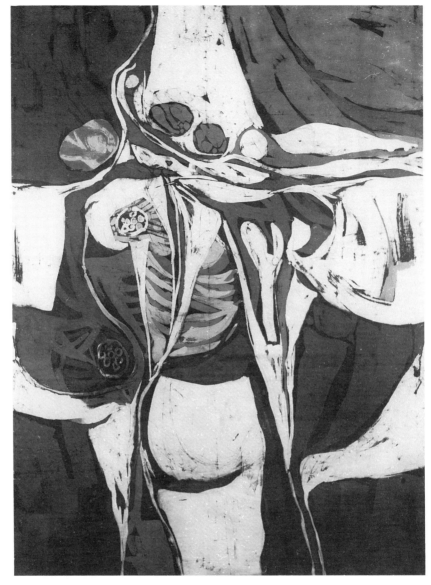

Figure 62   *Indian Summer* (detail). Batik on cotton.

able; only one brand is cited. Basic dyes are soluble in ethyl or de-
natured alcohol, as well as in water. The alcohol dries more quickly in
hand painting techniques. Recent formulations of these dyes have been
used successfully to dye acrylic fibers with improved light-fastness.

   BRANDS: Aljo Alcohol-water Basic Dye

Figure 63 *Bird of Fantasy,* 24" x 40". A stylized bird form in yellows and greens, with some red (Nancy Belfer).

APPLYING THE DYES

DYE BATHS

The traditional manner of applying the dye to the cloth is to immerse the entire fabric in the prepared bath of color. For the initial dye bath, the cloth should be handled very carefully so that the wax application is not disturbed. Light folding is best. First place the cloth in cool water for several minutes until it is evenly wetted out; then lift it out, allowing the excess water to drip off. The fabric can then be placed in the prepared dye bath for the correct length of time necessary to achieve the desired color. This is determined by tests made on small pieces of the same cloth being used in the batik.

A pan large enough to accommodate the entire fabric is necessary. The cloth should be gently moved about while in the dye bath so that the color penetrates evenly, without unwanted streaking. Wear rubber gloves while turning or lifting the cloth. Since the fabric will always seem much darker when wet, time the bath accordingly.

66

Review the rinsing procedures for the particular dye being used; for example, reactive dyes should not be rinsed until twenty-four hours have elapsed. When lifting the cloth from the dye bath, hold it over the pan so the excess dye drips back. If the color is not exhausted, the dye can be used again as a lighter value or it can be used as the basis for mixing a new color. Do not wring the cloth—this might break the wax. The rinse bath should be tepid rather than cold water.

After rinsing the cloth, spread it out to dry on newspapers or a sheet of plastic. It is also possible to hang the cloth to dry by fastening with clothespins on one end. Do not double the fabric over the clothesline as a streak will result at the line. If you use reactive dyes, always dry the cloth on a flat surface.

After the first color is completely dry, the cloth can be tacked once more to the stretcher frame. Examine the initial waxing carefully. It may be necessary to rewax or touch up some areas where unwanted cracking has occurred. If there seems to be an unusual amount of cracking, add more soft wax or beeswax to the formula.

At this stage the batik is ready for the second waxing. If sketching is necessary, use charcoal. Wax is now applied to all areas of the cloth that are to retain the first color. The brushes and tjanting tool can be used in the same manner as before. Check the back of the cloth to be certain the wax penetrates properly; it may be necessary to apply wax to the reverse side as well.

When the waxing is complete, prepare the second dye bath in the usual manner. It should be remembered that the second color will be affected by the first, and it should be selected accordingly. For example, if yellow is the first color, and red the second, the color obtained will be orange. In overdyeing, however, value as well as hue is important, so it is wise to make a preliminary test on a corner of the cloth to be certain the desired color is obtained.

This procedure of waxing and dyeing can be repeated several more times. The cloth is usually crushed before the last dye bath if a crackle effect is desired.

When you are working with dye baths, you should remember the following points:

1. Before entering the cloth, check the temperature of the dye bath with a thermometer.
2. If it is necessary to add additional dye to strengthen the dye bath, remove the fabric, add the pasted dye (never dry powder), stir thoroughly, and return the fabric.

3. For stronger color, allow the fabric to dry first, then rinse off excess dye and dry again.

4. Handle the cloth very carefully to prevent unwanted cracking and chipping of the wax.

If the batik is unusually large in size or on a very bulky fabric, such as velvet or wool, it may not be possible to find a pan large enough to accommodate it. If this is the case, the cloth can be dyed in sections. For convenience, this is best done on the floor or on a large table surface protected with newspapers. Fold the fabric lengthwise in half or in thirds and place one of the end sections in the dye bath, moving it about from time to time, until the proper color is obtained. Lift the first section out of the bath and put the next section into the dye, with a slight overlapping. Continue this until the entire fabric has been dyed.

It is important that all sections of the cloth be immersed in the dye bath for an equal amount of time; this insures uniform absorption of the color. This procedure can be quite time-consuming, but it is sometimes the only way a large or very bulky fabric can be properly dyed.

Allow the cloth to dry before rinsing out the excess dye.

Figure 64   The design for this batik wall panel was based on an arrangement of orange and watermelon slices (Gloria Smith).

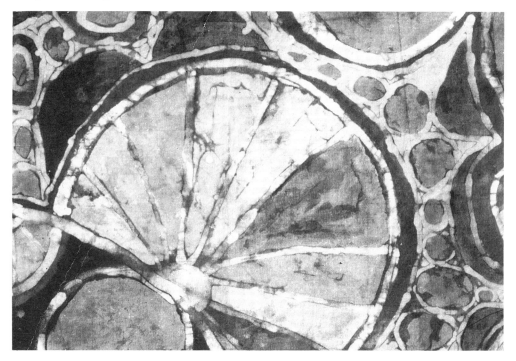

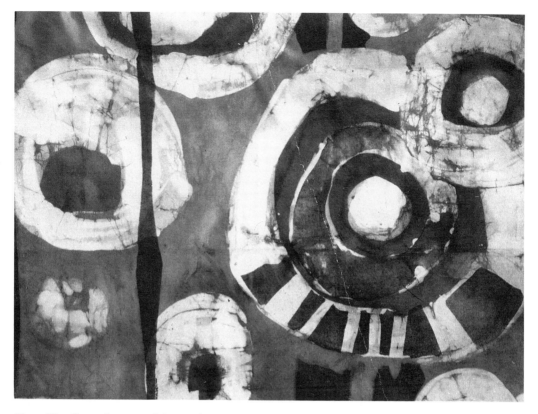

Figure 65   Strong forms, reminiscent of enormous flowers,
interrelate with lines in this detail of a batik wall hanging on cotton.

DIRECT BRUSH APPLICATION OF DYES

The application of the dyes with brushes, directly on to the stretched cloth, is a departure from traditional methods. After the initial blocking-in of shapes and lines with the wax, the colors are applied within areas of "islands" enclosed by the wax.

This is a technique that offers many possibilities in color usage, since several colors can be initially applied to the white cloth and when dry, retained with wax. Using the dyes in this manner allows for a more varied overall color imagery because the number of tonal variations possible through subsequent waxing and overdyeing is so much greater.

For example, after the first wax application, dyes in blue, green, and red can be brushed directly onto unwaxed shapes in the cloth. Each color is retained within a wax boundary. Some of the shapes can be left undyed, thus remaining white. When the dyes have dried completely, further wax applications can indicate additional variations in shape, line, and textural surface. At this stage, new colors

69

can be brushed on, or the entire fabric can be placed in a dye bath. A simple solution might be a dye bath of deep yellow: over the unwaxed red, orange would result; over the unwaxed blue, green would result; over the unwaxed green, yellow-green would result. Remaining areas of the cloth with neither wax nor dye will be dyed yellow. After drying, there could be additional waxing, controlled crackling, and a final dye bath in a dark color, perhaps purple or brown.

For brushing methods, the dyes should be strong concentrations that can be stored safely in covered jars. You can warm direct, acid, and all-purpose dyes before use if you insert an electric coil heater into the jar for a few minutes. Fiber-reactive dye solutions cannot be stored beyond a designated time span.

As the dye is brushed onto the different areas, check the underside of the cloth. On some types of fabric, the color will easily penetrate through so that both sides are evenly colored. If the color seems to be strong only on the top side, it may be necessary to brush additional color on the reverse side as well. This is most efficiently done by retacking the cloth to the frame with the back side up. If, after drying, the intensity of the color does not seem strong enough, the dyes can be reapplied in the same manner as before and allowed to dry.

When brushing methods are used, many soft but sturdy brushes are necessary, preferably one for each color. Good quality paint brushes 1″ or 1½″ wide with natural or synthetic bristles are satisfactory and can be purchased in hardware stores. Artists' brushes are not necessary. When the work session is over, the brushes should be carefully rinsed. The metal ferrule that holds the bristles will corrode in time if continually in contact with the dyes. The brushes will last much longer if the metal is covered with waterproof tape or masking tape as a protection.

Figure 66 *Acrobats* by Morag Benepe. Sculptural figures in batik on cotton velveteen.

It is also possible to apply the dyes directly to the cloth with small sponges or pieces of absorbent cotton rather than brushes. With paper stencils pinned to sections of the cloth, dyes can be sprayed on using an airbursh or small motorized paint sprayer. When dry, the wax is applied in the usual manner. Additional dye and wax applications will probably be necessary to develop the richness of the design.

It is also possible to thicken the dyes to control spreading of the color by using sodium alginate thickeners. To prepare a quart of medium thickener, mash 2 tablespoons of the granules with a small amount of rubbing alcohol; stir in the water and allow several hours to form a smooth gel consistency. Spoon off amounts as needed into the dye solutions for brush or sponge applications. There is no exact proportion for preparing the thickener; the amount of flow needed to achieve a smooth application can easily be adjusted.

Figure 67   Batik doll form by Morag Benepe.

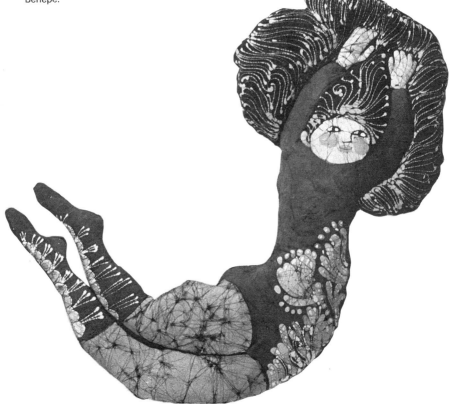

When dyes are used in warm rather than hot baths, as they would be for batik, a curing procedure is usually necessary to set the color. The ironing of the fabric for wax removal helps somewhat in this regard but a steaming of about one hour is also recommended.

Any large deep pot can be adapted for use as a steamer for this type of color fixation. The wide enamel kettles used to sterilize bottles are ideal. They are available in most hardware stores and are easy to use since the metal rack can be turned upside down to form a supporting shelf for the cloth. If a rack is not available, you can improvise a supporting grid by setting four tin cans of the same height around the bottom of the pot, evenly spaced. Then place a round, flat metal cake rack over the cans to form the shelf.

Place about fifteen to twenty layers of newspaper over the shelf. Measure the diameter of the pot and cut the circles of newspaper about one inch less. A circle of heavy felt should also be cut to the same size. Place the newspaper and felt on the shelf, centered, so that the sides of the pot are not touched. This will prevent splashing drops of boiling water from accidentally wetting the fabric.

The cloth should be lightly rolled in newspaper, then turned in to form a coil and lightly tied off. Unless printing pastes have been used there is no danger of unwanted color transferring from one layer of fabric to another, so it is possible to fold the cloth once or twice before rolling it in the paper. Keep the packet as loosely wrapped as possible to allow the steam to enter all layers of the fabric.

In a container of this type, about three to four inches of boiling water will provide steam for over one hour. Do not place the cloth bundle in the container until the water has boiled and the chamber has filled with steam. For a cover use a piece of thick carpet padding rather than the metal lid. The padding will absorb droplets of water and also allow the excess steam to escape.

When steam is in the container, remove the lid and quickly place the cloth bundle inside. If there is room several bundles can be steamed at the same time. Some additional pieces of felt or paper towelling can be put around the bundles. The lid should be returned to position as quickly as possible. The usual fixing time is for one hour but this time is often extended, especially when you are treating large or bulky pieces of fabric. If there is any doubt that the steam may not have circulated freely enough to evenly penetrate all layers of the cloth, you can rewrap the piece and repeat the entire process. After removing the fabric from the steam container, untie the cord and immediately remove the wrapping.

The steaming procedure is needed in particular for fiber-reactive dyes in direct applications, which require moist heat fixation methods to permanently set the dyes. The alcohol-base liquid dyes listed in the next chapter for painting on silk also require steaming. For extensive amounts of work, professional cylindrical steamers can be purchased from several dye suppliers which will accommodate large pieces of fabric.

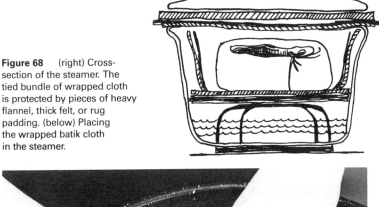

Figure 68 (right) Cross-section of the steamer. The tied bundle of wrapped cloth is protected by pieces of heavy flannel, thick felt, or rug padding. (below) Placing the wrapped batik cloth in the steamer.

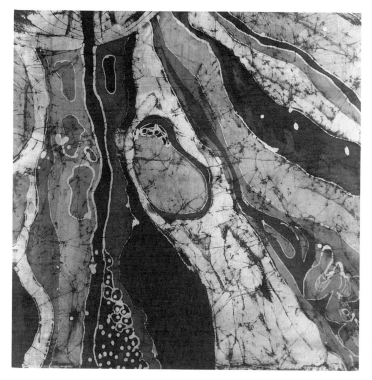

Figure 69 Detail of batik in which brush methods have been used to apply the dye (Lucille Licata).

ALTERNATIVE SETTING METHODS

STEAM IRON: Small to medium size pieces of batik fabric can be set by using a steam iron on a flat table or floor surface. There must be a sheet of clean, absorbent paper (newsprint, toweling) or a sheet of thin cloth both above and below the batik. For additional steam, use a soft, heavily dampened cloth, like cotton flannel, spread out as the first layer, followed by the sheet of paper, the batik, and the second sheet of paper. Iron for 10 minutes over each section of the fabric. Wait overnight before rinsing.

Note that this method, like the other setting methods, should be used after most of the wax has already been removed.

CLOTHES DRYER: Dyes will set after 1 hour in a commercial clothes dryer if the temperature is high enough, at least 180° F. Home clothes dryers are usually set at 150° F., so it is necessary to use a Laundromat dryer. This method can be used for batiks on lightweight cotton and silk which will not be subjected to extensive washing.

OVEN BAKING: Small batik pieces, as well as small pieces of painted silk, can be steamed in a kitchen oven with the temperature set at 285° F. The fabric is lightly wrapped in thin cloth, rolled up and tied, then placed on the rack in the preheated oven. Under the rack, a flat pan of boiling water provides the steam; the boiling water in the pan should be checked periodically for possible replacement. The steaming should continue for 15–30 minutes, depending on the weight of the fabric.

BATCHING: This is the method recommended for all tie dye techniques using fiber-reactive dyes, and will be described more fully in that chapter. The fabric (cotton, rayon) is first soaked in a bath containing soda ash. The dyes, mixed with salt and urea, are applied to the tied or clamped fabric. The batching method for setting the dyes calls for inserting the wet fabric in a plastic bag, which will keep it moist for 24–48 hours. The cloth is then rinsed to remove the excess dye, first in cool water, then hot, using Synthrapol detergent.

APPLIED FIXATIVE SOLUTIONS: Several dye suppliers carry fixative solutions which can be applied to the fabric as a soak or with a brush application. Some examples are Jacquard Permanent Dye Set Concentrate (soak) and Createx Fast Fix (brush application). Since these products are designated as compatible with specific brands of dye, suppliers' instructions should be consulted for details about their use.

DRY HEAT: Ironing with dry heat will only set pigment-base colors. Several brands are now available which can be used effectively for painting on silk as well as on thin cotton for the wax-outline batik method. Brands of pigment-based silk paints are listed in the chapter describing painting on silk.

Figure 70 *The Snow is Almost Gone* (9′ × 4′) by Dorothy Caldwell.
Discharge batik; wax resist on black cotton. Photo by Dan Meyers.

Variations on the Batik Process

PAINTING ON SILK

The technique popularly known as painting on silk refers to the direct application of dyes to silk fabric after the shapes of the design have been outlined with a resist. While many textile artists prefer the traditional resist of hot liquid wax, newer rubber-base resists have been developed which are considered easier to use for fine-line control. Regardless of the type of resist used, the lines of the design have a thin, delicate, flowing quality. The procedure is similar to the wax outline method in batik that is not taken to the final crackle dye bath.

Silk is an intrinsically beautiful fabric that is unusually receptive to dye coloration. Many types of silk are now available as yardage or in the form of scarves with hand-rolled finished edges. Suppliers of dyes frequently stock silk as well.

The type of silk most widely used for painting is habutae (habotai), a soft, smooth, lightweight fabric sometimes called China silk; it comes in different weights ranging from light to medium, 8, 10 or 12 mm. This fabric is the easiest to work with and is used extensively for decorative wall panels, silk banners, and unique, one-of-a-kind garments of all kinds. It is also recommended for the tie dye techniques described later.

More experienced artists may prefer other types of silk which can be used for more specialized effects. These are in a somewhat high price range and include silk woven in satin or twill patterns, broadcloth, crepe, and organza. A natural textured fabric in the same price range as China silk is silk noil, or raw silk. Since it is heavier than China silk, the liquid wax resist is most effective. A set of sample swatches is a good investment if you plan to do extensive work on silk.

Silk purchased for dyeing should already be degummed and will need only a gentle soaking in hot water with a small amount of mild soap for about one-half hour. Silk is a protein fiber, so avoid strong alkali detergents. Do not squeeze or wring the cloth. Allow cooling time, then rinse, adding some vinegar to the final bath. Hang to dry over a rigid rack. The cloth can be ironed while still damp. Some shrinkage should be expected.

Figure 71 Painting on silk, in progress; the dyes are brushed within the shapes outlined with gutta resist.

Figure 72 *Cosmopolitan* (36″ × 36″) by Yukie Orenstein. Hand painting with fiber-reactive dyes followed the *tjanting* tool application of wax in this figurative wall panel.

RESISTS FOR PAINTING ON SILK

The types of resists available for painting on silk offer different options relating to the choice of colorant and the method of setting the color. Both water-soluble and rubber-based resists are available which are applied to the silk using a plastic squeeze bottle with an applicator tip of plastic or metal to achieve a smooth, free-flowing fine line. Each type must be thoroughly dry before the colorant is applied; allow from **80** thirty minutes to over an hour, if necessary.

RUBBER-BASED RESISTS, called *gutta*, are thick, clear liquids very similar to rubber cement. This is the type of resist initially identified with painting on silk, because a thin, crisp line could be obtained on the fabric and it was much easier to control than the *tjanting* tool.

Gutta resists are available in the clear liquid as well as in metallic colors and black. After the colorant is set, either by steaming or dry ironing, depending on the type used, the clear gutta is removed by dry cleaning. The colored gutta remains permanently in the fabric. Solvent is needed for thinning the gutta and cleaning the applicator tips.

Unfortunately, the strong fumes of the gutta resists should not be inhaled, particularly over long periods of time, so if extensive amounts of work are planned, wear an approved respirator with a cartridge for fumes or vapors. Adequate cross-ventilation systems should also be considered. Individuals who are unusually sensitive to fumes should use water-soluble resists.

Gutta resists, when carefully thinned to a fluid consistency, will penetrate heavier weights of silk; too much thinning will weaken the resist. Some practice is necessary in adjusting the resist to the weight of the fabric, as well as in application, before adequate control is achieved.

BRANDS: Jacquard Gutta Resist
            Sennelier Gutta Serti

WATER-SOLUBLE RESISTS were developed as an alternative to the rubber-based resists, eliminating the solvent odor as well as the need to remove the resist by dry cleaning. These resists are non-toxic, odorless, and wash away in warm water after the dyes or paints have been appropriately set.

The water-soluble resists are also applied to the fabric with plastic applicators and penetrate readily if used on the lightweight grades of silk. The line is not quite as free-flowing as the gutta, and not quite as thin, but this is an acceptable alternative if used with the proper colorant.

The moist heat of steam-setting will soften most water-soluble resists, so these products work best when used with pigment-based colorants (silk paints rather than dyes) which are set by dry ironing. Apply the colorant up to within an inch or so from the resist line, allowing it to spread out naturally on the fabric. After the colors are dry and the ironing completed, most water-soluble resists wash away in a bath of warm water. Sennelier Resist Bien can withstand steaming and washes away in cold water.

BRANDS: Presist (Cerulean Blue)
              Sennelier Aqua Gutta
              Sennelier Resist Bien
              Deka-Silk Resist

COLORANTS FOR PAINTING ON SILK

The colorants available for direct painting on silk are of two distinct types: liquid dyes and pigment paints or silk paints. They differ in chemical composition and in the method used for setting the color. The dyes require steaming or soaking in a fixative bath; the pigment-base silk paints require ironing with a dry iron.

SILK DYES   are true dyes that penetrate and form a bond with the fiber. When correctly set, the colors are light-fast and washable. Dyes do not diminish the natural luster of the silk. The liquid dyes marketed for silk applications are of two types: liquid fiber-reactive dyes and alcohol-base liquid dyes, sometimes referred to as liquid acid dyes.

BRANDS: Couleurs Sur Soie (Textile Resources). Acid (alcohol).
              Createx (Color Craft). Fiber-reactive.
              Dupont French Dyes (Textile Resources). Acid (alcohol).
              Jacquard Silk Colors (Rupert, Gibbon & Spider).
                 Fiber-reactive.
              Pabeo Orient Express (Dharma). Fiber-reactive.
              Procion H (Cerulean Blue, PRO Chemical & Dye).
                 Fiber-reactive.
              Sennelier Tinfix (IVY Crafts). Acid (alcohol).
              Sennelier Super Tinfix (Dharma, IVY Crafts).
                 Acid (alcohol).

SILK PAINTS   differ from dyes in that they are pigment-based products that coat, rather than truly penetrate the fiber. The paints are thinned to simulate dyes and are sometimes called pigment-dyes, a confusing designation since the two colorants work in different ways.

Pigment colors can be used on all types of fibers, including synthetics, and are permanently set by ironing with a dry iron for several minutes. The pigment products prepared specifically for painting on silk are absorbed by the fabric evenly, if the area to be covered is not too large. Although the paints are not truly transparent, as are the dyes, they are effective on light weights of silk.

Silk paints are easy to use directly from the container and are compatible with water-soluble resists since they can be set with dry heat. The colors should be applied on the fabric up to about an inch from the resist line, allowing for the natural spreading of the color to touch the resist.

> **BRANDS:** Deka Silk (Rupert, Gibbon & Spider)
> PROfab Textile Inks (PRO Chemical & Dye)
> Sennelier Peintex (Dharma, IVY Crafts).

Figure 73 Reversible jacket by Kymberly Henson. Combined techniques of resist-dyeing, hand painting, and quilting, in silk jacquard. Photo by Jay Bachemin.

The step-by-step procedure for painting on silk using the gutta resist followed by the direct hand painting of the silk dyes.

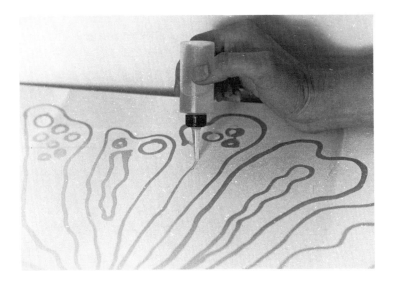

Figure 74   Applying the gutta resist.

Figure 75   As the resist dries, the shiny surface becomes dull.

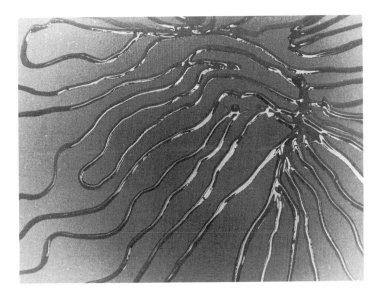

84

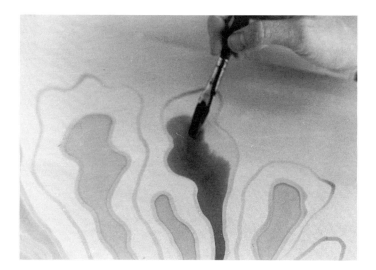

Figure 76   The dyes are brushed within the outlines of the resist.

Figure 77   The finished design, using seven different colors.

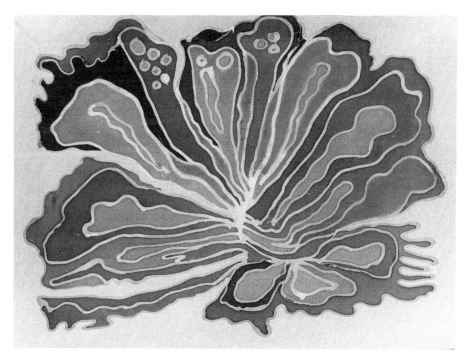

Figure 78 Resist-painted garments by
Kymberly Henson. (Above) *The Goddess
Within*, tunic and scarf in jacquard-
patterned silk. (Right) *Bandito*, jumpsuit
in crinkle-silk. Photo by Jay Bachemin.

Figure 79 Kimono-shaped top in silk broadcloth combines resist-dyeing and stencil-painting (Mieko Parwulski).

DESIGN CONSIDERATIONS

After some initial experimentation with the materials, the enormous range of design possibilities will become evident. The experience gained by practicing the technique on small samples leads to an accumulation of valuable resources in both skill development and design imagery. Frequently, what begins as a technical exercise or procedure becomes the means of projecting a personal direction in design that could not have been predicted beforehand.

Design inspiration can come from many sources. The imagination directs the translation of ideas into the medium. Combining techniques can also generate new ideas. In addition to painting on silk using the resists, the dyes can be painted directly without resists and blended on the fabric for watercolor qualities. Overpainting with opaque textile colorants which include metallic and pearlescent shades, can further highlight the expressive aspects of the design. The addition of other techniques, such as stenciling, block printing, appliqué, fabric pens, and embroidery, will create an interplay of rich surface effects in color and texture.

Tie Dye:
History and Tradition

The traditions in the dye-resist processes involving the tying, knotting, binding, or stitching of the fabric before dye immersion, are thought to be East Asian in origin. There are conflicting interpretations of evidence, however, that make a search for exact origins futile. There is reliable evidence of early knowledge of these processes in India, China, Japan, Java, and Bali. In Africa, the application of reserve dye techniques indicates abundant usage on utilitarian objects as well as textiles. The design motifs from Africa are very different from those found in Asia. Some of the earliest textile fragments found, however, come from Peru, and it is believed that knowledge of these processes spread from Peru into Mexico and the southwestern United States. Studies have indicated extensive applications of resist-dye techniques on the North American continent, owing to the widespread Peruvian influence, although there is greater continuity and more diverse application in the East Asian and Oriental civilizations.

Anthropologists have found that prototypes for simple resists are
found in all primitive cultures. The bleaching action of the sun may

have accidentally set off an awareness of a patterned surface obtained by a resist; from this realization, the concept of preparing material to resist coloration may have developed. Early tie and dye work on woven cloth was probably an adaptation of the ancient *ikat* technique, in which sections of the warp threads were bound off and tied before the weaving. *Ikat* has been known for centuries in Eastern Indonesia, especially in Bali. From using the resist-dye processes on warp or unwoven threads, the concept of designating sections of finished cloth for reserve dyeing seems a natural development. For hundreds of years these peoples have produced textiles of remarkable delicacy of pattern and rich ornamental appeal.

Traditionally, the process consists of isolating and firmly tying off small portions of the cloth in a carefully regulated manner. These sections usually formed a geometric arrangement of circlets and narrow stripes and are bound with natural fiber cords to form a protection from the dye coloration. After the dye bath, the cords are removed and the pattern emerges.

The most elementary patterns in tie and dye are the small circlets so prevalent on textiles from India, Sudan, parts of Africa, and Morocco. In spite of the technical simplicity of grasping and tying off a tiny segment of the cloth, many variations are possible. Large portions of the fabric can be reserved by incorporating specialized folding methods along with the binding. Circles, squares, and other geometric shapes can be gathered so that the flow of the folds converge at one point, with firm ties placed at intervals.

In the sewing or *tritik* process, prevalent in African textiles, a long, sturdy thread is stitched into the fabric along a predetermined line direction . . . straight, wavy, zigzag, etc. The cord is then pulled taut so that the cloth gathers. When the fabric is tightly bunched up along the line of the cord, it is tied off, forming the resist. The dye cannot penetrate the tightly enclosed gathers close to the cord.

All of these resist techniques have been known and practiced for centuries in the villages of India, especially in small centers close to large cities. A study of these fabrics is an introduction to the creative work of countless generations; cloth fragments have been found that go back 5,000 years. This folk or village tradition in Indian textiles reflected an expert knowledge of dyes. The saris, flared skirts, and head scarves, embellished with tie-dyed motifs, were in a range of brilliant colors, each hue associated with a symbolic meaning based on local customs and religious ritual. The images were geometric or highly stylized interpretations of familiar myths.

As in all traditional folk art, the degree of technical skill was amazing. The craftsmen were very carefully trained, often from childhood, in methods of working that were passed on from generation to generation. These were time-consuming skills, evident in the manner of preparing the thousands of tiny segments of cloth, all of which had to be carefully gathered and tied.

As in all folk crafts, industrialization has resulted in a breaking down of established traditions that have been practiced for centuries. In the textile crafts, this has meant a loss of indigenous design quality, as well as an impoverishment of the kinds of purposeful creative activity that are a wholesome and necessary part of personal and communal life.

Figure 80   Detail of a woven blanket from Indonesia in the *Ikat* or dyed warp technique. Before the cloth is woven, sections of the warp forming the pattern were carefully bound as a protection from the dye. After weaving, the resulting pattern appears blurred or slightly irregular.

Figure 81 Indian tie dye on silk. The small dots were bound with cord before dyeing. When the cords were removed, the dots appeared white on a red background. In the center black dye was brushed over some of the dots.

Figure 82 A similar technique on cotton. Photo by Buffalo Museum of Science.

Figure 83   This illustration shows Indian tie dye on silk, a controlled pattern of circular lines forming an allover floral motif. This crimped or creased surface is a distinctive quality of traditional tie dye work.

Figure 84   Indian tie dye on silk. This highly controlled pattern of a flower border and diagonal rows in the background was probably made by pressing the damp cloth into a wooden block with raised prongs defining the design. The ties are made using these prongs as a guide.

8 *Designing in Tie-Resist Techniques*

The tie-resist techniques described offer unique opportunities for a kind of color exploration attuned to the discovery of the relationship between the planned and the accidental. In some ways, the visual effects are closely related to the qualities of free watercolor painting, especially where transparencies through overdyeing occur. There can also be a distinct graphic quality.

The controls, obtained from the placement of the pleats, stitches, and ties, can never be thought of as an absolute means of predetermining the final visual result. It is suggested that the beginner try out the techniques described on small pieces of fabric, to be kept as references for future work on larger panels, realizing that there are too many variables for exact duplication. Changes in weight and size of the fabric, in the fiber content, in manner of pleating, in tightness of the bind, in the temperature and timing of the dye bath—all of these, and more, imply a variation in the resulting image.

There are, however, certain aspects of these techniques that can be planned, and a basic familiarity with these is essential for blocking 93 out placement and direction of shapes on larger pieces. The various methods of pleating are consistent in determining stripe directions: vertical, horizontal, diagonal, chevron, or squared. With the stitching and clamping methods, it is possible to control the placement and definition of both large and small shapes. The tritik technique is especially appropriate for those whose work temperament is inclined toward a more logical, predetermined surface rhythm.

Figure 85   In this section of a large panel in cotton muslin, the patterned surface results from random pleating, twisting, and tying. Direct dyes were used in brilliant yellows and blue.

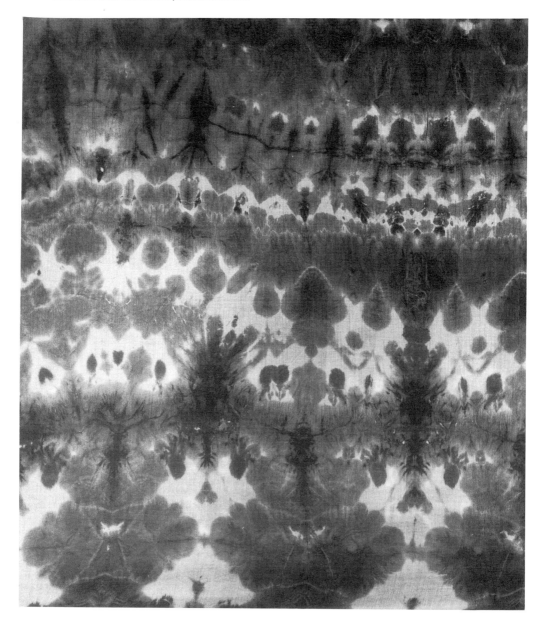

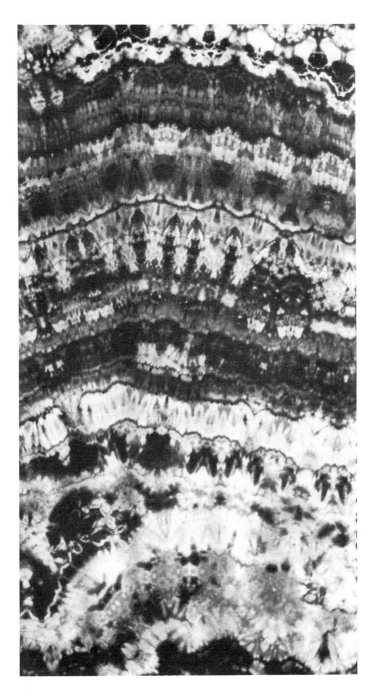

Figure 86 A contemporary tie dye by Carter Smith. Reds, oranges, green, and black were used in this vibrant wall hanging, 90" x 36".

It would not be wise for the beginner to settle too quickly into one particular mode of working or to give in so completely to the accidental effects that occur that all sense of planning is lost. The rewards of working in these processes come from learning to use the unpredictable effects to build more inventive design solutions. There is so much that can be discovered only by experimenting with an open awareness of "trial and error" possibilities. Often, an accidental effect can become the beginning of a new idea that will result in an increased sense of personal involvement. Working in these techniques over a long period of time gives the designer a deep understanding of the curious sense of balance between the planned and the unpredictable.

These ancient techniques offer countless ideas which the inventive contemporary designer can utilize in many different ways. Some elementary practice is usually all that is required to become familiar with the method by which the effects are achieved and to observe and build on the resulting pattern image.

9 *How to Make Your Own Tie Dye*

THE STUDIO: EQUIPMENT AND SUPPLIES

Working in the tie dye techniques calls for specific considerations as to space and facilities. Whether the studio is a room carefully set up for this purpose or a corner of the kitchen, an adequate, well-lit work space is necessary, with ample room to lay out the fabric and plan the folds.

Samples can easily be made using a small portion of a table or counter, but more ambitious projects call for a large work table or cleared floor area. If necessary, protect surfaces with plastic sheeting. There should be easy access to a sink, as well as a stove top or sturdy hot plate. Several enamel or stainless steel pans will be needed, in a variety of sizes. Keep spools and cut lengths of cord, rubber bands, and various small tools in separate boxes, readily at hand.

It is best to have everything assembled before starting to work. The following items will be needed:

cloth: cotton, silk
dyes: dye additives
measuring cups and spoons
pans: enamel, stainless
  steel, plastic
plastic squeeze bottles
cord, rubber bands
aluminum C clamps: 2″, 3″
items for clamping, two
  of each type

foam brushes, sponges
squeeze clamps
scissors, T pins
plastic bags, ties
rubber gloves
iron
plastic table protector
paper towels, newspapers
pencil, ruler

PROCEDURE

1. The fabric is prepared by washing (silk) or soaking in a soda-ash solution (cotton) which is not rinsed out.
2. The design is planned, designating the placement of the folds and the application of the bindings and clamps.
3. The dyes are prepared and applied to the fabric with plastic squeeze bottles or by immersion dye baths.
4. For cotton, allow newspapers to absorb excess dye, then seal the damp fabric in a plastic bag for 24–48 hours.
5. Rinse out excess dye with Synthrapol, open the bindings, and allow to dry. Repeating the fold, tie, and dye procedure is optional.

MAKING SAMPLES

The most enjoyable aspect of working in the tie dye techniques is in watching the shapes of color emerge as the cloth is untied and then unfolded. As you become familiar with the various methods of folding, typing, clamping, and dyeing the cloth, confidence will grow. This kind of confidence is an important factor in developing ideas of boldness and creativity. For those with little prior experience, it is suggested that the different techniques be practiced on small trial samples first.

Sample pieces of cloth should be both square and rectangular in shape and of the same fabric that will be used in larger projects. Try out all the techniques described and experiment with your own ideas to learn what will happen. There are some factors that can be controlled. At other times it is necessary to be receptive to accidents and learn to recognize their potential for building richness in the design. Save all the samples, with appropriate notes. They will become a fascinating resource for future work.

THE CLOTH

Many different kinds of cloth are suitable for resist-dye techniques. Fine- to medium-weight cotton, viscose rayon, or silk will be appropriate for all the processes described and are especially recommended for beginners. Heavier-weight cottons, as well as woolens, can also be used with some technical modifications. When purchasing cloth, be certain of fiber content and avoid cloth that has been treated with a soil repellant or crease-resistant finish.

Fabric yardage should be cut along a straight thread from one finished edge or selvage to another. It is important that all edges be aligned when pinning large pleats and folds.

Prehemmed silk scarves or silk yardage should be washed in a mild detergent, with some vinegar added to the final rinse. Cotton yardage, T-shirts, and other clothing should be given a preliminary soak in hot water with ½–1 cup soda-ash added to each gallon of water. Squeeze out and allow to dry without rinsing, as a preparation for using the fiber-reactive dyes.

BINDING AND TYING

Different kinds of cord and thread will be suitable for tying; choices should be made by considering the type of cloth used as well as the kind of resist that is wanted. Strength is an important factor. The material should not break easily under pressure of the ties.

On fine fabrics, thin cords, such as buttonhole twine or carpet thread, are excellent and can be used on silk, cotton lawn, thin muslin, and viscose rayon. Heavier cords, sold for package wrapping, can be used on medium-weight cloth. Raffia is also a fine material for binding and tying, especially effective on medium- to heavyweight fabric. Raffia will withstand absorption by the dye liquid, making for a very strong resist. Wide, sturdy rubber bands can be used when appropriate, as well as one-fourth inch rayon or nylon elastic, sold by the yard. Water-repellent cloth can be cut into one-half-inch strips and used for tying; plastic poly ikat tape is also excellent for bound resists since it is strong, flexible, and easily torn into strips.

The particular way that the cords are tied and the tightness of the bind determine the character of the resist. The cord must be wound very firmly if the dye coloration is to be kept out. If the cloth is slightly dampened, the ties can be made much tighter. Partial dampening can be achieved efficiently by spraying soft water

Figure 87   Front and back views of a dress in silk broadcloth combining tie-resist and clamping techniques.

(Calgon) onto each section. Use a bottle with a push-spray top, as those used originally for household cleaning solutions. Damp cloth will compress readily, allowing for a much firmer resist than can be obtained on dry fabric.

The cord can be put on in different ways to produce a variety of resulting patterns. When the cord is bound around the fabric in a very solid manner, closely filling the space, the dye will not penetrate the cloth. The resist can be strengthened by an additional layer of cord or raffia. When the cord is bound around the fabric in a widely spaced, crossover manner, the result will be a partial resist. Some dye will penetrate the cloth, forming an irregular stripe pattern. Often, when the cord is tied in this lattice manner, a distinct line appears in the resist image, imparting a very graphic quality.

Regardless of the manner in which the cord is bound, it must be fastened off securely if it is to hold in the dye bath. A tight double knot is best. If, after binding, one of the end cords has become too short for proper tying, attach a new length of cord by winding it several times around the former end (from the same direction) until it is tight and can be tied with the longer end.

Cutting the cords after dyeing requires unusual care because the cloth can be easily damaged. Usually it is possible to pull the knot away from the bound area and insert one of the scissor points. Do not use scissors that are too sharply pointed. After cutting, the cord is wound off, with additional clipping sometimes necessary. The cord can be saved, to be used again later.

Rubber bands are used in much the same manner as cords, except that their use is limited to areas of the cloth that can be reached within the grasp of the hand. They are stretched while they are wound and must be very sturdy or they will snap. Remove the rubber bands by any means that seems appropriate, pulling away or clipping.

The best time to remove bindings is while the cloth is still somewhat damp, about an hour away from completely drying. Once removed, the cloth should then be immediately ironed.

DYE APPLICATIONS IN TIE-RESIST TECHNIQUES

General information about different kinds of dyes available should be reviewed, since it is important to use a dye with an affinity for the cloth fiber. In tie-resist dyeing, the cloth is immersed in the dye bath for a relatively short period of time, usually about five to ten minutes. There can be instances, however, when one minute is sufficient (on thin silk) or when an hour or more might be necessary (on heavy wool) to obtain the required depth of color. Some caution is needed, since it is possible to destroy the subtleties of the resist by allowing the fabric to remain in the dye bath for too long a time. The bath can be lukewarm or hot, depending on the particular requirements of the dye. In preparing the dye bath, the objective is for a strong concentration that will provide the appropriate strength of color in as short a time as possible.

There are so many constantly changing considerations in tie-resist dyeing that it is not practical to try to work with exact proportions. Precise duplications are not easy to achieve, although with experience using one particular brand of dye, it becomes possible to predict results. The catalogs of several dye suppliers should be reviewed for specific recipes for tie dye applications. Both powder and liquid dyes can be used effectively; the recommended dye for cotton and rayon is fiber-reactive; acid dye is recommended for silk and wool.

The various categories of dyes generally available for studio use are described on pages 58–65. The information that follows is particularly relevant when you are working in the tie-resist techniques.

FIBER-REACTIVE DYES

The advantages of fiber-reactive dyes in tie-resist techniques on cotton and rayon are clearly evident from the brilliance of the colors and the fastness to light and washing. Used as recommended, steaming is not necessary; instead, a method called batching will permanently set the colors. The successful use of fiber-reactive dyes in tie-dye applications on cotton and rayon calls for the following steps:

PRELIMINARY FABRIC SOAK: A preliminary soaking of the fabric in a bath of hot water containing soda-ash is necessary as an aid in color fixation. Directions for different brands vary somewhat, with the proportions of soda-ash to 1 gallon of hot water ranging from ½ to 1 cup and the suggested length of time in the bath from 10 to 30 minutes. These differences are not critical. After the soaking, squeeze out the excess water but do not rinse. The folds, ties, and clamps can be applied to the fabric while it is still slightly damp or after it has dried.

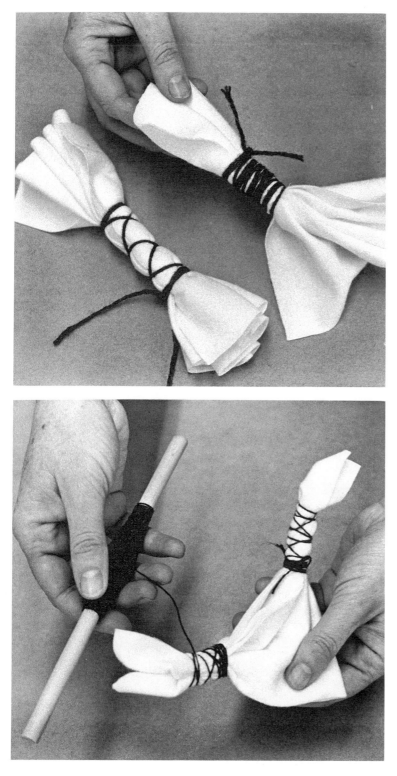

Figure 88 Samples with different methods of tying.

Figure 89 A squared cloth sample, folded into a triangle and tied at two corners. The cord is wrapped on a dowel stick.

DYE RECIPE AND APPLICATION: Since fiber-reactive dyes are available in both powder and liquid form, the recipes for solutions appropriate for tie dye will vary slightly with the brand selected; suppliers' instructions should be followed. For Procion MX in a 1-quart solution, 5–6 teaspoons of dye are needed for a medium shade; Createx Liquid calls for 4 tablespoons of the dye. The amount of dye is adjusted for the desired depth of color. The dye bath includes:

> 1 quart warm tap water
> Dye, in varying amounts, as needed
> 2 tablespoons salt (dissolved)
> 2 tablespoons water softener
> 4 tablespoons urea (optional)

The addition of urea, which aids in dissolving the dye and improving the depth of color, will make the dye more penetrating. The dye will creep rapidly along the threads, frequently under the bindings and clamps, blurring the resulting image. To counter this add a small amount of thickener to the dye to reduce the spreading. If sharp edges are wanted, experiment first with small pieces of the same fabric, taking special care to insure the tightness of the bindings and clamps.

Since soda-ash was present in the presoak, it is not included in the recipe; it can be added, however, if it is suspected that the amount in the

Figure 90 Sample showing one corner of the triangle dipped into the dye bath. Other colors can be used on the remaining corners.

presoak was inadequate. Consider using distilled water if the area tap water is highly chlorinated.

The dye solutions can be poured into plastic squeeze bottles for applications in selected sections of the folds, or used as baths for partial immersion dyeing.

BATCH SETTING AND RINSING: When the dye applications are completed, allow the excess liquid to be absorbed by layers of newspapers spread out on the work table. The fabric bundle is then placed in a plastic bag and sealed for 24–48 hours at room temperature or higher. The longer time is suggested for deeper colors.

When the sealed bag is opened, the cloth bundle is rinsed in cold water first, then in hot water to wash away the excess dye. Synthrapol detergent is highly recommended for the rinse baths to prevent backstaining, which is unwanted coloration on areas to be kept free of dye. The ties, bindings, and clamps can be removed while the fabric is in the rinse bath.

After the rinsing, squeeze out excess water and allow the fabric to dry on a flat surface. Ironing while damp, with a press cloth, will further set the dyes and remove crease lines from the folding. At this stage the design should be evaluated. The fabric can be considered complete, or it can be refolded and tied or clamped again for additional design variations and new dye applications.

ACID DYES

For tie-dye techniques on silk and wool, acid dyes are the most effective. While fiber-reactive dyes will work on silk in the hand-painting solutions containing baking soda, steaming is necessary for fixation; this is also true of the brands that suggest substituting an acid (citric acid, vinegar) for the alkali. A strong alkali, like soda-ash, is harmful to silk fibers. With acid dyes using hot baths according to the recipe on page 63, the steaming procedure is not necessary.

Silk is an ideal fabric for tie dye techniques. Since it is less bulky than cotton, it compresses easily and the ties, bindings, and clamps will produce sharp, clear images with the acid dyes. Colors will be clear and bright in both hot and warm dye baths, although a hot dye bath will give the best results in the partial dyeing methods used with these techniques. The hot dyes can also be poured into squeeze bottles for application in selected areas.

After the dyes have been applied to the tied or clamped fabric it is set aside and allowed to dry. The bindings can be removed while the fabric is still slightly damp and the cloth is then ironed to further set the dye. The fabric is then rinsed in cool water, allowed to dry partially, and then ironed again.

Used in hot dye baths, household or dual-component dyes can be applied in tie dye techniques with excellent results, and their ease of use makes them a practical choice under some circumstances.

For a variety of reasons, it may not be convenient to handle alkali or strong acid solutions. The brands and directions for tie dye are the same as described for batik on page 64. Since hot dye baths are possible, some brands can be used directly from the package without any additives. When required, the additives are salt for cotton and vinegar for silk.

These dyes work on both cotton and silk, both cellulose and protein fibers. The tie dyed fabric should not be subjected to hard washing or hung in direct sunlight for long periods of time.

PARTIAL DYEING

It is not necessary that the entire fabric be placed in the dye bath. The cloth can be designed with several stripes or shapes of different colors. Horizontal, vertical, chevron stripes, as well as folded and bound shapes, can be dyed as separate units. Large sections of multicolor striping can serve as a background for smaller, more detailed resist patterns.

Before placing the section in the dye bath, check the boundaries on each side of the color to be certain they are securely tied off. Since each color is dyed separately, care in handling is essential when you are removing the individually dyed sections from the bath. Plastic bags in various sizes, with ties, are excellent for protecting the remaining areas of the cloth from accidental spotting. While this method of dyeing is somewhat time-consuming, it offers numerous possibilities for inventive color exploration.

OVERDYEING

Much of the interest and variety in resist dyeing comes from overdyeing: that is, recoloring cloth that has been previously dyed. Usually, the fabric is folded again, then bound, stitched, or clamped to form a new resist image. A basic familiarity with color-mixing principles is important when overdyeing so that the second color chosen will effectively recolor the first. While there are no exact rules, a light or bright color is usually applied first, to be overdyed with another color of the same value or one that is more intense or darker.

After working with the dyes for a brief time, the effects of color mixing will be noticed. Often, when two dye colors are mixed together to produce a new color (e.g., green obtained by mixing yellow and blue) there will be a natural separation occurring on the cloth at places under the binding ties. The dyes penetrate the fibers at different rates and the more active color will extend out of the mixture into the gathered, folded, or tied areas of the fabric. These effects can often be predicted and can be utilized to great advantage in tie-dye work.

RANDOM EFFECTS

There are many ways of treating the cloth to produce random effects on the overall surface of the fabric. Preplanning is at a minimum with these methods; in fact, the attempt to plan is discouraged by the very nature of the procedures. These techniques are, however, an excellent introduction to tie-dye processes because they encourage spontaneous experimentation in handling and binding the cloth. In addition, they provide opportunities to become familiar with the dyes, both in color usage and in application.

The results, although unpredictable, are often very effective visually and should be evaluated as posibilities for additional work in folding, tying, tritik, and related techniques. The following suggestions will be most suited to thin fabrics, about 36 inches wide and 1½ yards long, or smaller.

1. Spread the cloth flat on a table surface. Grasp a section of the fabric with one hand. While holding the bunched-up cloth, wrap cord tightly around the area in a criss-cross manner. Without tying off the cord, grasp another section nearby and tie in the same manner. Continue this until the entire surface of the cloth has been bunched up and tied. The cloth can be sprayed lightly to dampen and additional ties can be made. The cloth can be dyed as follows:

   a. Dye in one color, a light value. When dry, additional ties can be made throughout the cloth. Then dye again in a more intense bath of the same color.
   b. Dye in one color. When dry, make additional ties and dye again in a new color.
   c. Dip the sections in several different colors. When dry, make additional ties and dye again in a new color.

Figure 91   Tying sections of cloth, gathered at random.

d. After dyeing according to method a or b, the fabric can be untied, ironed, and the entire process of bunching and tying can be repeated with a different placement. The fabric is again dyed.

2. Fold the cloth in half and make a series of unmeasured vertical pleats or gathers. Holding one end firmly, begin twisting the entire length of the fabric with the other hand. On lengths of over a yard it is more practical to clamp down one end or have another person hold it while the twisting is being done. As the twisting becomes very tight, the cloth will seem to coil on itself. Bring the two ends together, allowing the coils to form naturally. Tie the two ends together first, and then place a few additional ties around the coils. The cloth can be dyed in any of the methods suggested above.

3. Tie objects into the cloth in a random placement. Dowel rod pieces of different lengths are especially effective in producing circular patterns in the cloth. Insert the piece of doweling into the

cloth and smooth the fabric around it from the point to the base. As the cloth gathers toward the base of the rod, try to distribute the bulk evenly. Bind first at the base, while holding the gathers firmly. Then place additional ties at intervals along the dowel piece, either as a solid bind or in a criss-cross manner. Repeat this procedure throughout the cloth, using the different lengths of doweling.

The fabric can be dyed in any of the previously suggested methods. Procedure c as listed above will be especially useful, resulting in very rich overdye effects in the circular patterns.

Different kinds of objects can be tied into the cloth, as well, each resulting in a distinctive pattern image. Pieces of wood lattice stripping, wood or plastic thread spools, buttons, and washers are all suitable.

Figure 92   In this wall hanging by Carter Smith, several tie dye techniques are utilized in the circular motif centered in a background of brilliant red.

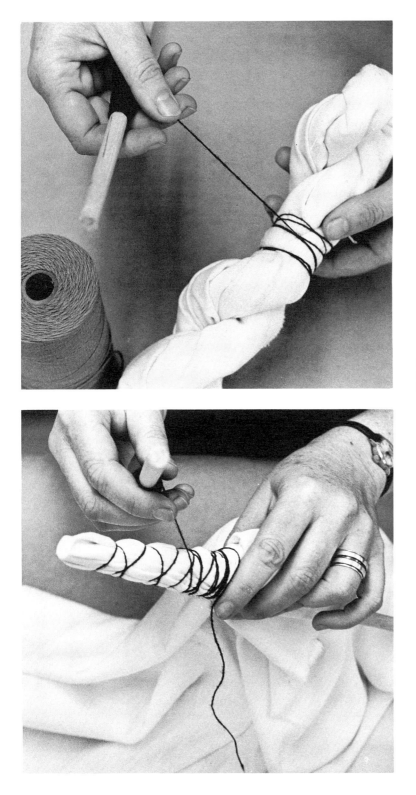

Figure 93 A twisted and coiled length of cloth is tied intervals.

Figure 94 A dowel stick tied into the cloth.

Figure 95   This design was produced by random pleating and tying around a one-half-inch diameter dowel rod inserted in the center of the cotton fabric.

METHODS OF FOLDING

On long sections of cloth, the basic fold technique is an accordion-like type of pleating extending from one end of the fabric to the other. This pleating, combined with additional folds and bindings, will result in many effective patterns. The width of each pleat, as well as the number of pleats that can be formed, will be determined by the weight of the fabric. A thin, soft fabric can be folded many times, while a heavier fabric will naturally be more suited to fewer pleats. Fine cloth can be folded in half first and then formed into the pleats.

It is possible to measure out each pleat for precision in placement. To do this, the cloth is placed on a flat table surface or on the floor while the pleats are measured with a yardstick and marked with a pencil. As each pleat is formed it is held in place with pins or paper clamps, until all the pleating is completed.

It is not necessary that all the pleats be of the same width. Variations in spacing can occur at any time. For example, wide pleats can be placed at the center, gradually becoming narrower toward the selvages of the fabric. Or, just the reverse can be planned, with the wide pleats at the edges and a gradual narrowing at the center. The procedure for measuring and pinning is the same. After the initial lengthwise pleating is completed, the fabric can be tied at intervals and dyed.

Variations in folding techniques occur when, in addtition to the lengthwise pleating, more folding is done along the pleated section. These techniques are most effective on thin fabric or small pieces. If a full width fabric is used, the spacing of the pleats is usually wider—perhaps four or five inches apart—than the spacing on a narrow length of cloth.

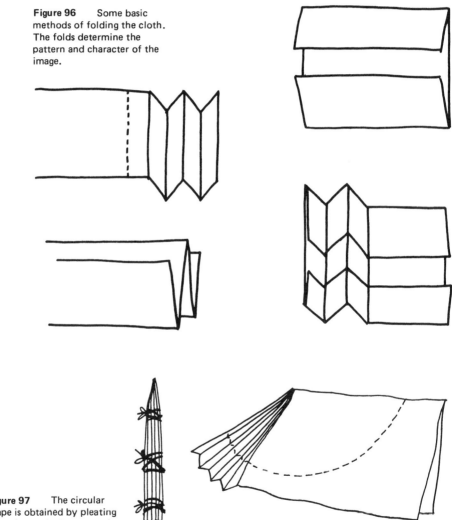

Figure 96 Some basic methods of folding the cloth. The folds determine the pattern and character of the image.

Figure 97 The circular shape is obtained by pleating from the marked center point.

Figure 98   Image formed by controlled pleating and tying.

Figure 99   Image formed by controlled pleating and tying.

On a rectangular piece of cloth, the lengthwise folds or pleats are made first and pinned into place. Then, additional pleating or folding can be done in a number of different ways.

1. The pleated length of cloth, taken as a whole, is folded from one end to the other in a series of evenly spaced pleats. The resulting packet of cloth is then tied in the center. Since many layers of cloth are in the bundle, the ties must be very firmly made. Raffia or wide rubber bands are excellent. If the cloth is damp, a tighter bind can be made. Before dyeing, pull apart the exposed pleat edges to allow the dye to be evenly absorbed. The dyeing can be done as follows:

   a. The entire bundle is dyed one color.
   b. One end of the bundle is dyed one color, the other end in another color.
   c. To introduce additional variation in pattern and color, after the initial dyeing, the entire folding and tying procedure can be repeated on a slightly different alignment. The second dyeing method can be either a or b, as listed above.

2. Fold the cloth in four or six pleats lengthwise. One end of the pleated cloth, taken as a whole, is folded from one of the corners diagonally over to the opposite side, forming a triangle. This diagonal folding is alternately repeated for the remaining length of the cloth. Work on a large table surface so the fabric can be conveniently turned for each fold. The resulting packet will be triangular in shape. Using rubber bands or raffia, bind the two corners following the long side of the triangle. This method will produce a diamond-shaped pattern, the number of points determined by the number of lengthwise folds. Dye in the methods described above.

3. For a chevron stripe or zigzag effect, fold the cloth in half and lightly mark a series of diagonal lines from the center fold down to the selvage sides. The lines should be parallel, about two to four inches wide. Carefully form pleats along the lines, holding with pins whenever necessary. The cloth will form a long, narrow strip. Tie at various intervals, and dye. When the cloth is rinsed and partially dry, add additional ties and dye a second color. For two chevron stripes, fold-pleat the cloth in four sections.

METHODS OF FOLDING SQUARE SECTIONS OF CLOTH

A square section of cloth lends itself to techniques of folding that utilize the four even sides of the cloth; the resulting pattern is based on the square format. Although all the folding methods suggested for rectangular sections of fabric can be used on squares, there are several techniques of folding that are especially appropriate for this shape. Again, where measuring and marking is called for, it should be done with a yardstick and pencil. For some of the folds, it may be necessary to mark the exact center of the square with a dot.

The following suggestions for folding utilize the square to advantage.

1. With the center of the square marked, fold the cloth in half. Form a triangle by bringing the corners at the fold up and into the center of the cloth, as shown in the Fig. 115. Pin the triangle in place, then pleat or gather at random from one side of the triangle to the other. Tie and dye in one or more colors.

2. Bring each corner in to touch the center dot, pin in place. A smaller square shape will result. Fold this in half, with the point edges on the outside. Gather and tie at various intervals. Dye in one or more colors. Realign ties and dye again.

3. Fold the square in half and then in half again. Using this as the basis, experiment with many different ways of gathering, folding, and tying.

Figure 100 Clothespins, straight pins, paper clips and clamps are some of the tools used to hold the cloth in place while making the ties.

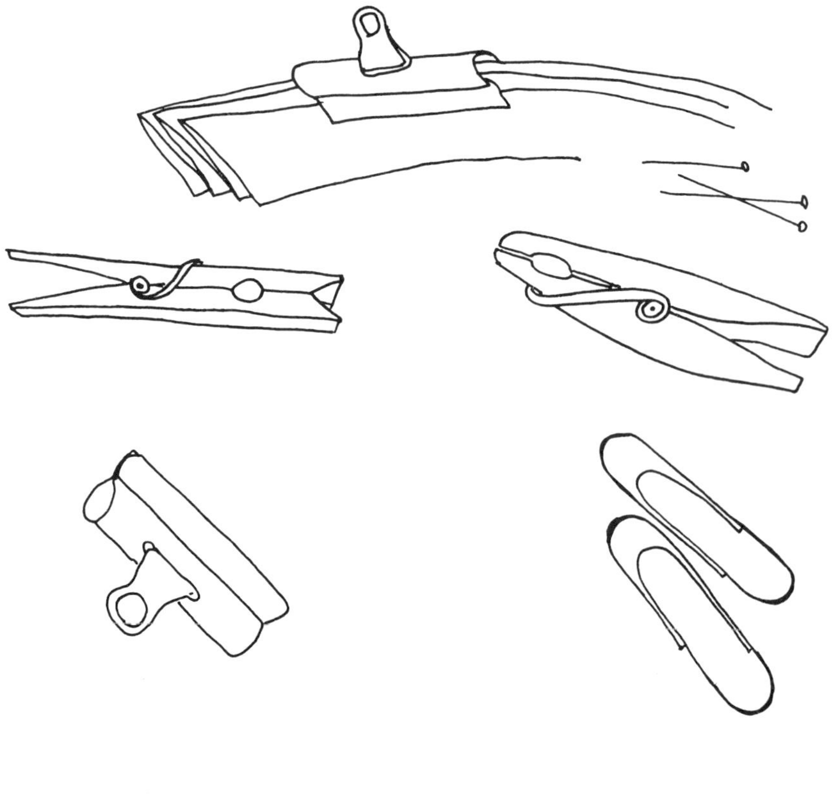

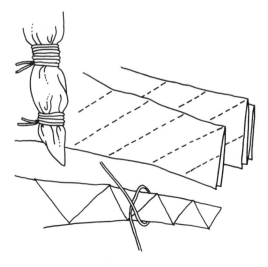

Figure 101 Folding and tying procedure for the chevron stripe.

Figure 101   (cont.)   Chevron stripe.

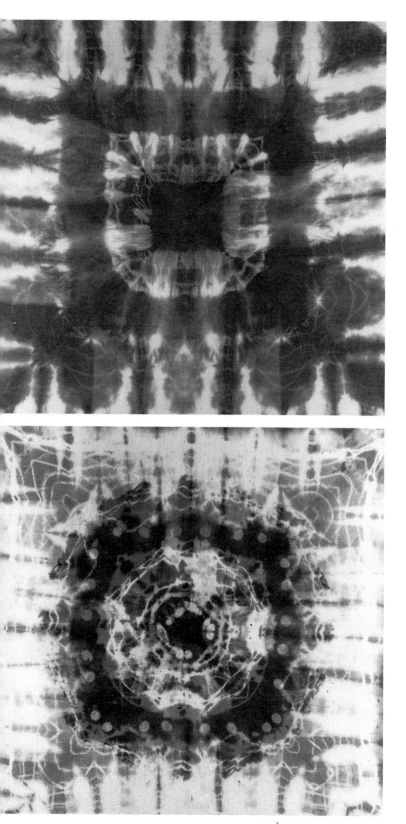

Figure 102   Patterns on square sections of cloth.

Figure 103 Detail of pattern of a folded and tied square cloth.

Figure 104 Illustration of method #1, for folding and tying a square section of cloth. The resulting pattern fits within the square format.

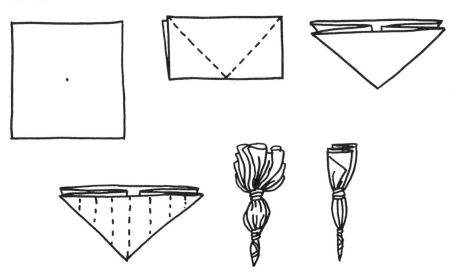

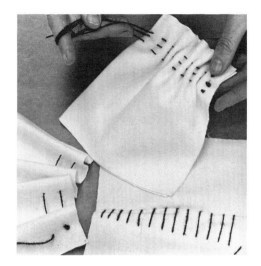

Figure 105   Samples showing
various methods of stitching.

TRITIK

Many kinds of strongly defined shapes can be dyed into the cloth using the tritik or sewing technique. It allows for a great deal of versatility and because of the control possible, a very personal kind of imagery can be developed if you combine this method with the various folding, binding, and clamping techniques. The stitches can be made on unfolded as well as folded cloth.

No real knowledge of sewing in the dressmaking sense is necessary, because these methods are extremely simple in themselves; the complexity comes about in the designing. Any fabric suitable for tie dye can be used, ranging from lightweight to heavy—although a more effective resist can be obtained on a lighter-weight cloth. The size of the needle, the cord, and the length of the stitch will depend on what is appropriate to the type of fabric being used. Embroidery needles, long, sharp, and with a large eye, are ideal for tritik. Ordinary sewing thread, doubled, is suitable for working on silk and thin cottons. On medium- to heavyweight fabric, use carpet or buttonhole cord. The size of the cord is not as important as its strength; if it breaks easily do not use it.

The stitch most frequently used in tritik is called the running stitch: a consistent over and under passing of the needle through the cloth. The length of the stitch can vary from about ¼" to ½". A very sturdy knot should be made in the cord before beginning the stitching.

The basic procedure is to use the stitching to outline the shape, then gather or tightly pull up the threads and firmly tie off the ends to hold the gathers in place. The sewing can be done on a single thickness of cloth, or, where a symmetrical spacing is planned, the fabric is folded from edge to edge. The method of dyeing is similar to that used in the other resist techniques.

Before applying the tritik technique to large panels, several variations should be tried out on small lengths of cloth (¾ to 1 yard square), which can be kept as reference samples.

1. Stripes: a straight line of running stitches, gathered, tied, and dyed, will produce a textured linear band in resist. Parallel rows of stitches will form an overall textural surface. Curved lines, as well as zigzag line formations, can be stitched in this manner.

2. Shapes: specific shapes can be outlined in tritik to obtain a resist against the background. If a strong image is planned, it will be necessary to reinforce the shape outline by adding several more parallel rows of stitches.

3. Tucked pleats: make a pleat or tuck in the cloth about one to two inches deep. Pin in place and stitch along the base of the pleat with running stitches. Expand this idea to a series of parallel tucks, or tucks following curved, pointed, or diagonal lines.

Figure 106   Forming a circle with two rows of running stitches.

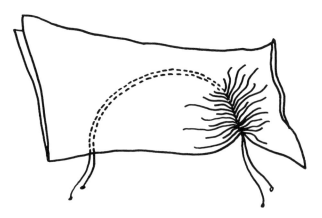

Figure 107   Approximate placement of some of the stitches for the wall hanging shown in Fig. 108 and the appearance of the cloth after the threads have been pulled.

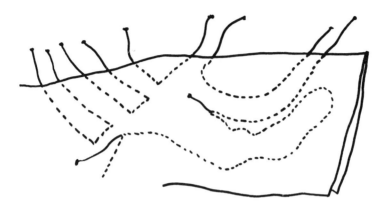

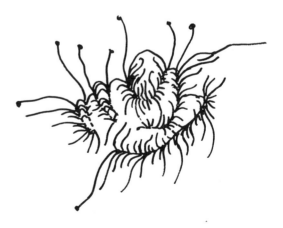

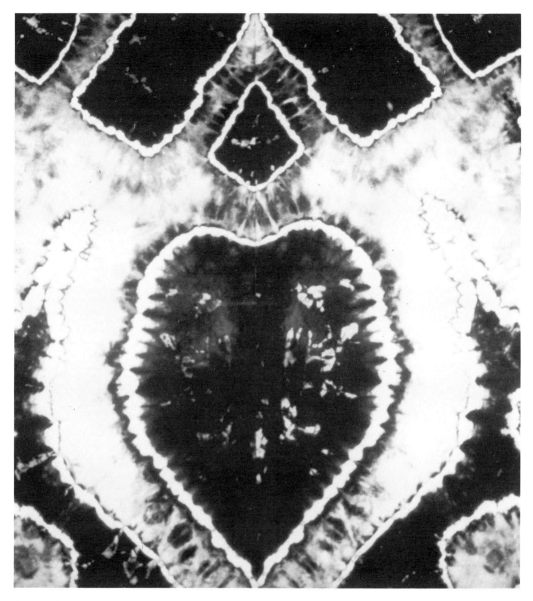

Figure 108   Detail of a wall hanging by Marian Clayden using tritik and tying techniques on silk.

CLAMPING METHODS

A reinterpretation of a Japanese technique called "jamming" allows for the dyeing-in of very clearly defined shapes. The principle involved is that of tightly clamping several layers of cloth between

124

two solid blocks which form the resist, protecting the cloth from the dye. The blocks can be of any shape and made of any material not affected by immersion in the liquid dye baths. Rigid sheet plastic, nonrusting metal, one-fourth inch plywood, or masonite board can be used. Wood and hardboard can be cut on a jig or band saw without too much difficulty; the pieces should be sanded and coated with shellac for protection. Geometric shapes of 18-gauge copper are available from commercial suppliers. Galvanized washers of different sizes, purchased in hardware stores, can also be used as resists for clamping.

A very sharp distinct resist can be made using the clamps. The technique is best suited to fine- or medium-weight fabrics that can be tightly compressed; any fabric, however, properly handled, can be adapted to this method. When planning the design, it is important to remember that the more the fabric is folded with more layers of cloth between the clamps, the greater the chance of a hazy, indistinct resist. A fine fabric, such as China silk, can be pleated into from ten to twenty layers with clear results, while a medium-to heavyweight cloth can only be pleated to form six to ten layers. Initial tests on small pieces of the material are helpful before planning the design. The fabric should be sprayed damp before clamping.

The clamps used must also be impervious to repeated dippings in dye liquid. Aluminum C-type clamps are most practical. Although the aluminum clamp is about twice as expensive as the common castiron type, it is a necessity for serious work in this method. It is important that enough clamps be placed on the template to insure an adequate resist. The heavier the fabric and the larger the size of the resist shape, the greater the number of clamps necessary. Small washers can usually be held with one clamp. Each clamp should be tightened as far as possible.

After clamping, the cloth sections on each side of the resist can be refolded, bunched, tied, or knotted in any number of different ways, depending on the character of the overall image. Clamping can be used on undyed cloth, creating a white resist, or on cloth that has been previously dyed with stripes or other appropriate backgrounds. The clamped resist will be in the first color and the area surrounding it in the second color produced by the overdye.

The dyeing procedure is similar to that of the other resist methods, but a somewhat larger vessel may be needed to accommodate the clamps. If the resists are used only in one section, protect the remaining cloth with a plastic bag. After the dye bath, place the fabric on newspaper for a time, rinse, and allow to dry.

When the cloth is almost dry, loosen the clamps and remove the templates and whatever other cords and bindings were used. Unfold the fabric and iron, first warm and then at the appropriate temperature for the cloth.

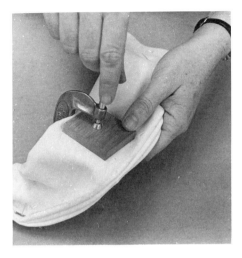

Figure 109 Clamping the pleated cloth between two wood blocks.

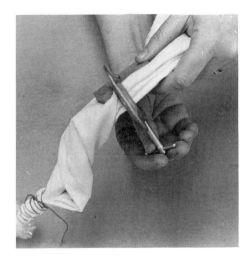

Figure 110 Clamped section placed in the dye bath. At left, a hand clamp holds the rim of a plastic bag which protects the rest of the cloth from dye splashes.

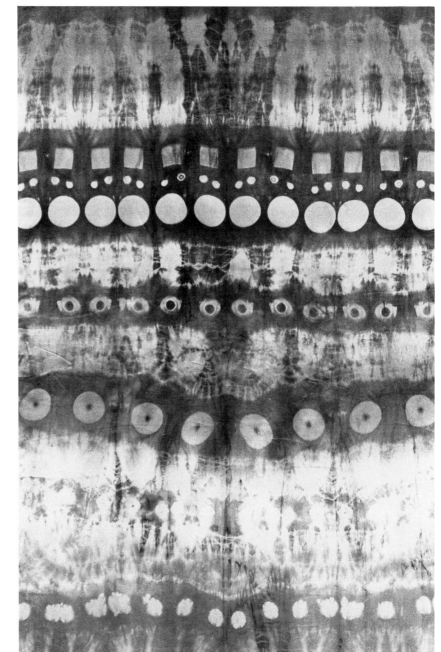

Figure 111   Wall hanging on satin using clamping techniques as well as pleating and tying methods.

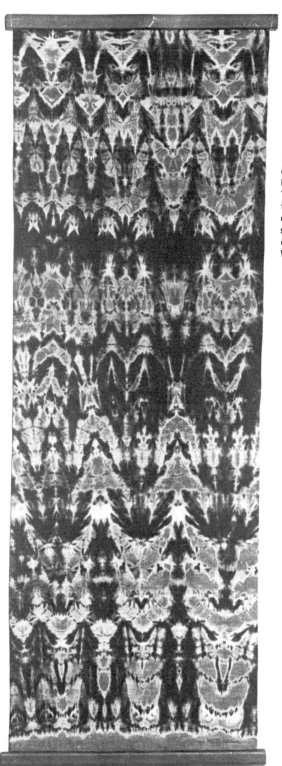

Figure 112 *All Creatures Great and Small.* Wall hanging by June M. Bonner. Technique: resist fold and tie—discharge. Material: cotton. Color: black and shades of brown. Collection of Mr. and Mrs. William E. Ward.

Figure 113   *Old Man Stone and Child Stone* (17″ × 19″) by Dorothy Caldwell. Batik discharge technique on cotton. Photo by Dan Meyers.

DISCHARGE DYEING

A variation on the standard tie and dye procedure, and one well worth exploring, is discharge dyeing. In this method, the color is removed from the cloth, rather than added, with the bindings and ties serving to protect the original color of the fabric. All the techniques described for use on white cloth can be utilized in discharge dyeing; the difference is that the fabric is a very dark or very intense color. In addition to folding and tying, sewing and **129** clamping methods can be used successfully.

To remove the color, immerse the fabric in a chlorine bleach solution. For discharge methods, first test a small piece of the cloth in a chlorine solution to be certain that the color will actually bleach out. Many commercially dyed fabrics are resistant to bleaching and cannot be used. Inexpensive cotton remnants are more likely to be satisfactory in this regard. If there is some rayon content in the cloth, the color may bleach out, but not to white. Black, for example, may bleach to orange or brown; dark blue may bleach to gray or pink. These results are impossible to predict in advance but can be most effectively used with these techniques. If suitable fabric cannot be purchased, it is possible to dye a length of cloth in the usual manner, rinse, dry, and then use it as a base for the discharge dye methods. A safe solution is:

1 part household bleach
2 to 5 parts water

The bleaching action will be faster if a stronger solution is used, such as half water and half chlorine bleach, but caution is necessary since there is a danger of weakening the fibers. Careful, timed testing is important. Use chlorine bleach only on cotton and rayon; it will permanently damage silk and wool fibers.

The procedure is as follows:

1. Test a sample of the fabric to ascertain the best proportional mixture of chlorine bleach and water.
2. Plan the design and determine which resist method will be used.
    Batik discharge: apply the hot wax with brushes, *tjanting* tools, cut blocks, found objects, etc.
    Tie dye discharge: after folding the fabric, place bindings, stitches, clamps, etc. in selected areas.
3. Wet the entire cloth or the portion to be bleached.
4. Immerse the fabric in the bleach solution. Wear rubber gloves and move the fabric about continually so the bleaching action can be clearly observed.
5. When the correct amount of bleaching has occurred, remove the fabric and place it immediately in a prepared rinse bath or hold the cloth under running water. A cup of vinegar in the rinse bath will neutralize the chlorine bleach.
6. Wash the fabric in hot water and detergent to completely remove the bleach. The addition of water softener to the last rinse will help in decreasing the chlorine odor.

This work should be done in an open, well-ventilated area. Sometimes the chlorine fumes are irritating, so frequent fresh air breaks are necessary. Always wear rubber gloves; the bleach in full strength should not touch the skin.

Commercially prepared color removers such as thiourea dioxide can also be used, but these require hot simmer baths and are more appropriate for removing the color from yardage lengths rather than for use with tie dye techniques. The hot simmer bath will melt the wax if used in batik discharge methods. Considering ease of use and safety, the best option for discharge techniques in both batik and tie dye is liquid chlorine household bleach.

With an understanding of the technical aspects of a medium, the first step has been taken. Understanding and doing, however, go hand in hand. Possibilities have been presented, but only by doing and, therefore, by actually using these possibilities, can individual confidence and creative growth occur. It is hoped that in addition to technical knowledge, the joy and challenge of working in batik and tie dye has been conveyed, as well.

Figure 114 Details of images resulting from discharge dyeing.

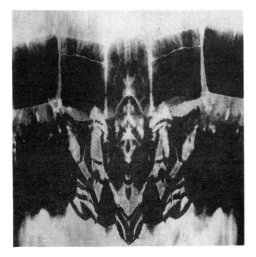

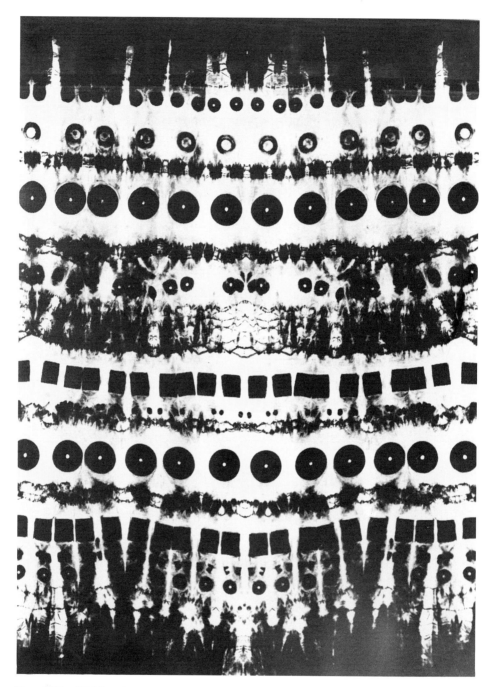

Figure 115 Wall hanging on cotton using discharge methods with pleating, clamps, and tying.

Figure 116 Rows of heart shapes and large dots are stamped in a repeating pattern arrangement in this batik from Turkey on red cotton with black dye.

Figure 117   Water-soluble resists were applied in this batik on cotton forming a simple repeating pattern of stylized floral shapes.

Glossary

Acid dyes. A category of dyes intended for use on protein fibers (wool, silk, and other animal fibers) as well as nylon. Acetic acid is used proportionally to exhaust the dye bath.

Affinity. The term used to describe the compatibility of a dye to the specific fiber content of fabric or yarn.

Assistant. Any substance added to a dye bath or hand painting solution that facilitates the bonding action of the dye and fiber.

Baking soda (sodium bicarbonate). A mild alkali used with fiber-reactive dyes in hand painting solutions to activate the dye.

Basic dyes. A category of dyes intended primarily for use on silk and wool. The colors are unusually brilliant but are not lightfast.

Batching. A procedure for setting fiber-reactive dyes by keeping the fabric sealed and damp for 24–48 hours prior to rinsing.

136

Batik. A method of resist dyeing in which hot, liquid wax is applied to the fabric in areas not to be dyed. After several wax and dye applications, the wax is removed.

Cellulosic fibers. Fibers derived from plants or regenerated plant materials, such as cotton, linen, jute, and viscose rayon.

Crackle. In batik, the fine weblike network of lines over the surface of the cloth, caused by cracks made in the wax before immersing the fabric in the dye bath.

Direct dyes. A category of dyes with affinity for cellulosic fibers: cotton, linen, viscose rayon.

Discharge. The removal of color from fabric through the application of a bleaching agent, either in liquid or paste form.

Dye. A natural or synthetic substance that colors yarn or fabric by chemically bonding with the fiber.

Dye bath. The proportionate mixture of water, dye, and appropriate additives to achieve coloration on immersed fabric or yarn.

Exhaust. The gradual chemical action in an immersion dye bath that results in the absorption of the dye by the fiber.

Fastness. The relative degree of exposure to light and washing a fabric colorant can withstand.

Fiber-reactive dyes. A category of dyes for cellulosic fibers with the highest ratings for wash and light fastness; a permanent chemical bond forms between the dye and the fiber.

Fugitive color. Color that is not fast to light and/or washing.

Gutta. A solvent-based liquid resist used for painting on silk.

Hand. Refers to the feel of the fabric when handled, its relative drapability or stiffness.

Household dyes. Dyes that contain portions of two distinct dye categories, direct and acid, enabling them to be used successfully on both cellulose and protein fibers.

Hydrolize. With fiber-reactive dyes, a portion of the dye reacts with the water rather than the fiber, causing a loss of color depth; the use of a water-softening agent is helpful.

Ikat. Pattern or design in woven fabric obtained by binding off or tying selected portions of the warp and/or the weft threads to resist dye applications, prior to weaving.

Mercerization. The mill process of treating cotton yarn or fabric with caustic soda to increase dye affinity and strength.

Mordant. A substance applied to natural yarn or fabric to create an affinity between the fiber and certain types of dye.

Overdyeing. Dyeing over a previously dyed yarn or fabric to strengthen or change the color.

Pasting (dye). Dissolving powdered dye by mashing it in a small amount of water prior to preparing the dye bath.

pH scale. The scale, from 0–14, measuring the relative acidity or alkalinity of a dye bath. Neutral pH value is 7; less than 7 indicates more acid, higher than 7 indicates more alkalinity.

Pigment. The coloring substance in an ink or paint, requiring the addition of a binder and vehicle for application.

Plangi. The Malaysian term referring to different types of tie dye techniques.

Protein fibers. Fibers derived from animal sources, including various types of wool (hair fiber) and silk (filament fiber).

Resist. A substance or material (heated wax, tight binding, clamps, etc.) placed on yarn or fabric to prevent dye from reaching preselected areas, resulting in a pattern or image.

Salt. A dye assistant used in dye baths for most types of dye to insure level dyeing and uniform depth of color. Plain table salt can be used.

Shibori. The Japanese term for tie dye resist techniques on textiles.

Soda-ash (sodium carbonate). Alkali used to activate fiber-reactive dyes; also used in laundering as washing soda.

Sodium alginate. A product derived from seaweed used to thicken dye solutions for direct hand painting applications.

Steaming. A process of setting the dye in hand painting applications by steaming the fabric for a predetermined length of time.

Stripping. The chemical removal of color from dyed yarn or fabric.

Tie dye. A method of resist dyeing in which selected portions of fabric are folded, tied, and/or clamped to resist subsequent dye applications.

Tjanting. A tool for applying hot wax to fabric, consisting of a reservoir to hold the wax, a spout through which the wax flows, and a handle.

Tritik. A textile-resist technique requiring a series of stitches sewn into the cloth, which are gathered and fastened off to form a protection from the dye.

138 *Urea.* A moisturizing agent used with fiber-reactive dyes in hand painting solutions to improve color yield.

Water-softener. An agent (Calgon, Sequestrant, etc.) that is added to water in dye baths and hand painting solutions to enhance the absorption of the dye into the fiber by deactivating the minerals in the water.

Wax formula. The proportionate amounts of paraffin and beeswax (or soft industrial wax) used as a hot resist in the batik process.

Directory of Suppliers

W. Cushing & Co.
P O Box 351
Kennebunkport, MA 04046
207 967 3711

Cushing brand "Perfection" Dyes.

Dharma Trading Co.
P O Box 1916
San Rafael, CA 94915
800 542 5227

Brands: Dyehouse Procion; Pabeo
Orient Express; Sennelier. Dyes,
silk paints, large selection of
clothing, fabrics by the yard. Catalog with instructions.

Earth Guild
One Tingle Alley, Dept T
Asheville, NC 28801
800 327 8448

Brands: Deka, Lanaset Acid dye,
Procion, Sennelier. Resists, tools.
Folder with product descriptions.

FabDec
P O Box 3811
San Angelo, TX 76904
915 653 6170

Brands: Procion (powder & liquid).
Cotton fabrics. Resists, tools. Directions with order.

IVY Crafts Imports
5410 Annapolis Road
Bladensburg, MD 20710
301 779 7079

Sennelier brand liquid dyes for
silk; silk paints. Resists, fabrics,
silk scarves. Folders with product
descriptions.

Lauratex Fabrics
153 West 27th Street
New York, NY 10011
212 645 7800

Fabrics: cotton fabrics in various
weaves, by the bolt only.

PRO Chemical & Dye Co.
P O Box 14
Somerset, MA 02726
617 676 3838

Brands: Procion, Cibacron, Ciba-
Kiton acid, PRO acid, liquid Fiber-
Reactive. Additives, resists.
Folders with instructions.

Rupert, Gibbon & Spider, Inc.
718 College Street
Healdburg, CA 95448
800 442 0455

Brands: Deka, Jacquard, Procion.
Dyes, silk paints. Large selection
of silk, rayon, and cotton fabrics.
Catalog with instructions.

Savoir Faire
P O Box 2021
Sausalito, CA 94966
(Write for information)

Brands: Sennelier products, dyes
and silk paints. Opaque and iri-
descent paints. Folders with product information.

Silkpaint Corp.
P O Box 18-F
Waldron, MO 64092
816 891 7774

Silkpaint brand paints for silk.
H. Dupont silk dyes. Folders with
product descriptions.

Sureway Trading Enterprises
826 Pine Avenue, Suite 5–6
Niagara Falls, NY 14301
416 596 1889

Fabrics: silk yardage, prehemmed
silk scarves.

Testfabrics
P O Box 420
Middlesex, NJ 06846
201 469 6446

Fabrics: large selection of fabrics
in all fibers, ready for dyeing and
printing. Fabric sample swatches.

Textile Resources
123½ Main St.
Seal Beach, CA 90720
213 431 9611

Brands: Deka, Ciba-Kiton acid
dye, Couleurs Sur Soie, Dupont
French dye, Procion. Folder with
product descriptions.

Thai Silks
252 (T) State Street
Los Altos, CA 94022
800 722 silk

Fabrics: large selection of silk
fabrics, yardage, prehemmed
scarves, clothing. Brochure available.

Bibliography

HISTORICAL BACKGROUND

Blakemore, Frances. *Japanese Design Through Textile Patterns*. New York: Weatherhill, 1978.

Donahue, Leo. *Encyclopedia of Batik Designs*. Philadelphia: Art Alliance Press, 1981.

Elliott, Inger McCabe. *Batik: Fabled Cloth of Java*. New York: Potter, 1984.

Gittinger, Marielle. *Master Dyers to the World*. Washington, DC: The Textile Museum, 1982.

Jefferson, Louise. *Decorative Arts of Africa*. New York; Viking, 1973.

Korwin, Lawrence. *Textiles As Art*. Chicago: L. Korwin, 1990.

Langewis, Laurens. *Decorative Art in Indonesian Textiles*. Amsterdam: C. P. J. Van der Peet, 1974.

Kubota, Itchiku. *Opulence: The Kimonos and Robes of Itchiku Kubota*. New York: Kodansha, 1984.

Larsen, Jack Lenor, *et al. The Dyer's Art: Batik, Ikat, Plangi*. New York: Van Nostrand Reinhold, 1976.

Lubell, Cecil, ed. *Textile Collections of the World. Vol. I, II, III*. New York: Van Nostrand Reinhold, 1975, 1976, 1977.

Polakoff, Claire. *Into Indigo: African Textiles and Decorative Arts*. Garden City, NY: Anchor Press, 1979.

Robinson, Stuart. *A History of Dyed Textiles*. Cambridge, MA: MIT Press, 1969.

Schevill, Margot. *Costume as Communicator.* Seattle, WA: University of Washington Press, 1986.

Sieber, Roy. *African Textiles and Decorative Arts*. New York: Museum of Modern Art, 1982.

Spring, Christopher. *African Textiles*. New York: Crescent Books/Crown, 1989.

Textile Designs of Japan. Compiled by the Japan Textile Color Design Center. New York: Kodansha, 1988.

Warming, W., and Gaworki, M. *The World of Indonesian Textiles*. New York: Kodansha, 1981.

Wheeler, Monroe. *Textiles and Ornaments of India*. New York: Museum of Modern Art, 1964.

TECHNICAL INFORMATION

Barsky, N., and Tuchman, D. *A Complete Guide to Silk Painting*. Booklet available from IVY Crafts Imports.

Blumenthal, Betsy, and Kreider, Kathryn. *Hands on Dyeing*. Loveland, CO: Interweave Press, 1988.

Dryden, Deborah. *Fabric Painting and Dyeing for the Theatre*. New York: Drama Book Specialists, 1981.

Hollander, Annette. *Decorative Papers and Fabrics*, New York: Van Nostrand Reinhold, 1971.

Jerstorp, K., and Kolmach, E. *Textile Design Book*. Asheville, NC: Lark Books, 1988.

Johnson, Meda Parker, and Kaufman, Glen. *Design on Fabric*. New York: Van Nostrand Reinhold, 1967.

Kanzinger, Linda. *Complete Book of Fabric Painting*. Spokane, WA: Alcott Press, 1986.

Knutson, Linda. *Synthetic Dyes for Natural Fibers*. Seattle, WA: Madrone Publishers, 1982.

Lambert, Patricia, *et al. Color and Fiber*. West Chester, PA: Schiffler, 1986.

Maile, Anne. *Tie Dye as a Present Day Craft*. London: Mills and Boon, Ltd., 1963.

Meilach, Dona. *Contemporary Batik and Tie Dye*. New York: Crown, 1973.

Nakano, E., and Stephens, B. *Japanese Stencil Dyeing: Paste Resist Techniques*. New York: Weatherhill, 1982.

Peverell, Susan. *The Fabric Decorator*. Boston: Little, Brown, 1988.

Proctor, R., and Lew, J. *Surface Design for Fabric*. Seattle: University of Washington Press, 1984.

Tomita, Jan and Noriko. *Japanese Ikat Weaving*. Boston: Rutledge & Paul, 1982.

Vinroot, S., and Crowder, J. *The New Dyer*. Loveland, CO: Interweave Press, 1981.

Wada, Y., Rice, M. K., and Barton, J. *Shibori: The Inventive Art of Japanese Shaped Resist Dyeing*. New York: Kodansha, 1983.

FILMS

Batik. 12 minutes.	Aims Media
	626 Justin Avenue
Tie Dye: Designing with Color	Glendale, CA 91201
15 minutes.	213 240 9300

VIDEOS

Fabric Painting on Silk and	The Unicorn
Cotton with Candace Crockett.	1304 Scott Street
90 minutes.	Petaluma, CA 94954
	800 289 9276

Note that dye suppliers' catalogs often list additional instructional videos demonstrating specific products in various project applications.

PERIODICALS

American Craft
40 West 53rd Street
New York, NY 10019

Fiberarts
50 College Street
Asheville, NC 28801

Shuttle, Spindle & Dyepot
120 Mountain Avenue
Newtown, CT 06470

Threads
Taunton Press
63 S. Main Street, P O Box 5506
Newtown, CT 06470

Index